What Leaders Are Saying about This Book

"Parents of teenagers need help, hope, and how to's. Dave Veerman delivers all three. Parents want to hear from someone who has 'done it,' and Dave's done it. Drawing wisdom from decades of ministry to teens, principles from his intimate familiarity with God's good Word, and illustrations from his own real-world experience as a father, Dave has written a solid field manual for parents. Chapter 5 alone—'Pump Up the Volume!' which deals with music and entertainment—is worth the price of the book."

Stu and Linda Weber
FamilyLife National Speakers Team
authors of *Tender Warrior* (Stu) and *Mom! You're Incredible* (Linda)

"I remember watching *The Adventures of Ozzie and Harriet* when I was a boy. I always wondered why my parents weren't as 'cool' as they were. But then, my family lived in the real world—a world that was different not only from Ozzie and Harriet's TV world but also from the world we live in today. We parents face some tough challenges that neither Ozzie and Harriet nor our parents had to face.

"I am grateful that Dave Veerman has had the courage to tackle a number of very difficult issues that all of us must face in today's real world. He draws not only from his own experience as a parent but also from the experience of others, resulting in a book of solid, practical advice. I highly recommend this book to all parents who want to succeed with their kids."

Wayne Rice
Director, Understanding Your Teenager Seminars
Cofounder, Youth Specialties
author of *Enjoy Your Middle Schooler*

"Not only did I enjoy this book for its relevant content, practical suggestions, and strong message to parents of teenagers—of which I am one—but I *know* and *trust* the author as a person deeply committed to both God and kids! Who could ask for a better voice to listen to and a better teacher from whom to learn?"

Becky Tirabassi
parent, speaker, author of *Let Prayer Change Your Life*

"We have had the privilege of parenting five through the teen years, and we found the process to be extremely rewarding and encouraging. Without question each day confronted us with decisions, questions, and challenges. Our regret is that we didn't have the book or counsel of Dave Veerman during those years. He has provided practical insight covering many of the pressure points, including entertainment, television, friends, church, and, of course, money and jobs. We recommend that you buy and read this book. It's a good investment. We wish we had had it earlier."

Ron and Judy Blue
Ron is managing partner of Ronald Blue & Co.
Ron and Judy are the authors of *Raising Money-Smart Kids*

"This book gives invaluable counsel. In a day when we are experiencing a continued decline in values among young people, this book provides solid direction to parents who have to make important but tough choices. We parents want our kids to grow and mature into being responsible Christian adults who help make a difference in the world. That's the goal of this book, and I highly recommend it to you."

Dr. John M. Perkins
publisher of *Urban Family Magazine*

Ozzie & Harriet

HAD A SCRIPTWRITER

Making Tough Choices with Your
Teens in the Real World

BY

DAVID R. VEERMAN

Tyndale House Publishers, Inc.
WHEATON, ILLINOIS

Library of Congress Cataloging-in-Publication Data

Veerman, David.
   Ozzie and Harriet had a scriptwriter : making tough choices with
your teens in the real world / by David R. Veerman.
      p.   cm.
   Includes bibliographical references.
   ISBN 0-8423-4786-0 (hc : alk. paper)
   1. Family—Religious life.   2. Parenting—Religious aspects—
Christianity.   3. Child rearing—Religious aspects—Christianity.
I. Title.
BV4526.2.V43   1996
248.8′45—dc20   95-39471

Printed in the United States of America

02   01   00   99   98   97   96
8   7   6   5   4   3   2   1

I dedicate this book to Tom and Julie Essenburg,
great friends and encouragers and terrific parents,
committed to Christ, strong, loving, and willing to
make the tough choices

Other Books by David R. Veerman

101 Questions Children Ask about God
102 Questions Children Ask about the Bible
103 Questions Children Ask about Right and Wrong
From Dad with Love with Chuck Aycock
Getting Your Husband to Talk
Getting Your Kid to Talk
How to Apply the Bible
On Eagle's Wings
One Year Memory Book for Families
Parenting Passages
Reaching Kids before High School
Reaching Out to Troubled Youth with Dwight Spotts
Ready for Life
Serious Fun
Small Group Ministry with Youth
Video Movies Worth Watching
Youth Evangelism

CONTENTS

FOREWORD

My life as David Nelson on *The Adventures of Ozzie and Harriet* did follow a script. And it seemed so simple, especially when we look back on the television show from our perspective as parents living on the edge of the twenty-first century.

The problems Rick and I had on the show seem so tame compared to the problems our teenagers face in today's world. In some ways teens haven't changed—they are still trying to discover their identity and are just reaching out trying to experience things. The problem is that today's avenues of experience can be very dangerous—from drugs to sexual activity to everything else.

Dave Veerman is right. Teenagers need strong parents who will stay involved with their teenagers, who will give firm guidance, who will not be afraid to set boundaries and stick to them.

As I look back on my years as the son of the off-screen Ozzie and Harriet, I am grateful that my parents set strict boundaries. My father was very conscientious. His father had died when he was twenty-one years old. My father put himself through school and worked very hard. Most people don't know that he was an attorney. He graduated from Rutgers Law School, was a member of Phi Beta Kappa, and was head of the debate team at Rutgers University. That made it a bit tough on Rick and me, because if we got into an argument, we had to make sure we had our facts straight. Our father was not about to let us get away with sloppy thinking.

My father would often remind us, "There are no freedoms without boundaries." That saying was one of what Rick and I called "Ozzieisms." What my father meant was that we all will need to do things we don't like to do. We are not free to do just the things that we enjoy doing. We must all pay our dues.

My parents expected a lot from us. My life was a bit different from other teenagers' lives because I grew up in Hollywood, but my parents tried hard to give us as normal a life as possible. I went to school; I was involved in sports and other activities—just like other kids my age. At times it felt strange that after school I had to go to work on the set while it seemed that everyone else got to go play around. But in other ways working on the television show was a tremendous advantage. We had our parents with us all the time. We saw them in action, and they had an opportunity to model to us the values that were important to them. Working on the show gave me a strong sense of responsibility, which certainly helped later in my life.

While my parents gave us boundaries, they also gave us latitude. If something my father had written or allowed in the show was particularly embarrassing to us, he would always listen to what we had to say.

Rick and I knew our parents cared for us. I remember one night when Dad, Rick, and I were playing basketball out in the yard. I'm not quite sure what prompted my father to say this to us, but he said, "You know, you guys can come to us with any problem that you have. Even if you told us that you had killed someone, it wouldn't change our love for you." That was a thunderbolt for me. I certainly was not thinking of ever killing anyone, but he used that extreme to tell us that no matter what we did, he and our mother would still love us and care for us. That impressed me.

My father set a powerful example for us. Not only did he care about us, he also cared about his wife and a lot of other people along the way. He helped a lot of people. He always gave 100 percent, and he expected that of us in all areas, whether in grades, sports, or whatever. That's all he expected. It wasn't a question of success or failure as long as we had given our best. He didn't expect any more or any less from us than he was able to give. He would say, "Listen, everyone is inherently lazy, and it's something we all have to fight for the rest of our lives. You have to establish your values and say what it is that you want to achieve and give it 100-percent effort."

Parenting is hard today. During the past decades parents had a hands-off approach, allowing their kids to do whatever they wanted. I don't think children want that kind of freedom. I think they want structure.

When my children were teenagers, I took comfort in knowing that God is our Father. I like to think of him as part of our extended family. I've learned that as a Christian, if I can't find a solution for something, I can lean back on the fact that God is our Father, and I can turn over my problem to him. I have found great direction and strength in the truths of the Bible. When I was a parent of teenagers, I could say, "I want you to do this not because I'm me and I'm your parent. I want you to do this because it's what the Bible says is the right thing to do." The truths of the Bible have lasted for centuries. They are worth our consideration.

I would encourage parents of teenagers to let your teens know that you care for them—no matter what. Set an example for them, and be there for them when they have to make the tough choices. In the end, trust God as the ultimate Father.

David Nelson
Hollywood, California

ACKNOWLEDGMENTS

Special thanks to these youth-ministry veterans who provided invaluable insight and counsel for this project.

Rick Bundschuh, author and copastor at Kauai Christian Fellowship (Kauai, Hawaii); Ridge Burns, Director, Center for Student Missions (San Juan Capistrano, California); Jack Crabtree, Executive Director, Long Island Campus Life (New York); Kara Eckmann, Director of College Ministry, Lake Avenue Church (Pasadena, California); Bill Jones, author, speaker, and president of Crossover Communications (Columbia, South Carolina); Len Kageler, Chair, Department of Youth Ministry, Nyack College (Nyack, New York); Daryl Lucas, author, editor, and father of three boys (Wheaton, Illinois); Al Menconi, author, speaker, and expert on youth culture (San Marcos, California); David Olshine, Director of Youth Ministries, Columbia International University (South Carolina); Wayne Rice, speaker, author, and cofounder of Youth Specialties (San Diego, California); Bill Sanders, youth speaker, author, and TV host of *Straight Talk* (Kalamazoo, Michigan); Len Woods, Minister to Students, Christ Community Church (Ruston, Louisiana).

Thanks also to David Nelson, for sharing his reflections about growing up in the Nelson family and for sharing his insights about the importance of being strong parents.

INTRODUCTION

The decade of the fifties saw the emergence of rock 'n' roll, teenagers as a sociological class, and the "golden age" of television. It was the time of bobby socks, "Rock around the Clock," crew cuts and ducktails, and the "peace, progress, and prosperity" Eisenhower years. Coming after Korea and before Vietnam, protests, riots, assassinations, Watergate, and the information age, this decade of innocence and optimism engulfed my early adolescence. I remember when Dad brought home our first television set. Soon watching television became a family event as we gathered around the set on the weekends.

One of my favorite shows was *The Adventures of Ozzie & Harriet.* Weekly, the Nelsons, "America's favorite family," would make their appearance in glorious black and white. In each lighthearted half-hour episode, Harriet and Ozzie would dispense insightful advice to solve David's and Rick's latest dilemma. The Nelsons, a close and loving family, would eat meals together (even breakfast), have fun together, and talk things over regularly. They represented much of what family life was supposed to be like.

More than four decades later, I find myself in Ozzie's role as a family man, the husband of one and father of two. But the nineties seem so much more complex, with computers, drugs, and powerful media influences. I long for life to be as simple as my memory and those television shows portrayed it. But I have to remember, Ozzie and Harriet also had a scriptwriter.

You and I don't have a script for parenting our children. Life for us is very complex, filled with a steady stream of tough choices. And no one makes more tough choices than parents do. At no time in the parenting process are parents more challenged than when their children move toward adolescence. Beginning in junior high, kids face an avalanche of pressures and temptations that seem to escalate each day. They are inundated with broadcast messages from music, movies, videos, and MTV. At the same time, these preteenagers and teenagers are growing rapidly, transforming into young men and women; they want to act *older*, and they look the part.* Pressured by media, peers, and their changing bodies and minds, these kids challenge parental authority and push the limits. Parents wonder how to respond, what to permit, and when to say no. These are years of tough choices.

- Your seventh grader wants to date. What will you tell her?
- Your high school junior wants to have a part-time job during school so he can buy a car. Do you let him?
- The cable company offers an unbelievable deal on a package of television entertainment options. Will you take it?
- Your eighth-grade daughter asks if she can go to an R-rated movie with her best friend. She assures you that the friend's parents approve. How will you respond?

Some parents take the easy way. When confronted with an important decision or ethical parenting dilemma, they try to ignore the problem, pretending it doesn't exist and hoping it will

---

*The word *teenager* in this book will take on a bit broader meaning because I would like to include the two preteen years. In effect, the term *teenager* refers to anyone in either junior high or high school. To avoid confusion, the book will use the terms *junior high* and *middle school* interchangeably.

disappear. Other parents, lacking the courage of their convictions, simply give in. Tired of arguing, they look the other way.

Melissa, an attractive sixth grader, has been using makeup and wearing short skirts to school lately. Her dad has expressed concern, but her mom thinks she looks cute. Both parents assume that everything is fine; their little girl is just becoming a young woman.

Now in the second year of middle school, Dennis has watched his grades take a nosedive. Instead of studying, he seems to spend most of his time with his friend Sammy or with his eyes and mind riveted on video games. Until this year Dennis was consistently on the honor roll. His parents don't seem too worried, however; they have decided that Dennis is just going through a stage and will snap out of it.

Tall and handsome, Ben has become the party animal of the junior class. Every young woman in school would love to date him, but he belongs to Kristie. Every weekend they go out, usually to a party or a show. Ben's mother, a single parent, figures she can trust her son. He's a good kid. Besides, she has enough to worry about, working a full-time job and caring for the two younger kids.

Whenever you see Clarice, you hear her music. She is continually plugged in to her favorite CD or radio station. Her collection of CDs must be larger than that of any other fifteen-year-old in the state. Her parents allow her to listen to whatever she wants, as long as she keeps her door closed and keeps the volume down.

In all of these families, the teenagers need strong parents who will guide firmly in love, draw the line, say no, and help them survive adolescent pressures and temptations. They need parents who are willing to spend the energy to make the necessary, tough choices.

This book explores ten critical areas about which teenagers and their parents need to make choices:

1. Friends—helping choose positive relationships
2. Dating—reacting to pressure to couple up
3. Personal faith—resolving conflicts over church
4. Media—controlling the influence of television
5. Entertainment—providing positive alternatives to popular music and movies
6. Values and priorities—dealing with jammed schedules
7. School—balancing grades and extracurricular activities
8. Money and jobs—teaching financial responsibility
9. Talents and abilities—discovering and affirming hidden talents
10. Future—broadening perspective and encouraging a forward look

These ten issues are guaranteed not only to cause conflict between parents and their teenagers but also to provide opportunity for growth and learning. Each of the ten chapters in this book focuses on one of the ten critical areas. Each chapter is divided into three major sections: *challenge, conflict, choice.* The challenge section sets up the problem issue; the conflict section describes how the issue influences the parent-child relationship; and the choice section explores how parents can hold the line and make the tough choices. A final section in each chapter lists questions to help parents analyze their parenting style, evaluate their teenagers' decision making, and plan a strategy to correct weak or faulty patterns. I encourage you to take those questions seriously. Keep a journal or notebook, and jot down your reflections and responses to those questions.

As you read these chapters, some of them will hit the mark with you. You will think, *Yes, this is exactly what my teenager is going through.* That may be especially true of the first five chapters, which deal with issues common to all teenagers. The final five chapters—chapters that deal with busy schedules, the value of education, money and jobs, exploring hidden talent, and preparing for the future—may apply to some parents but not others. Or they may apply to one of your teenagers but not the other. Each kid is different.

On the other hand, you may read these chapters and think, *I wish I had done that with our kids earlier. Now it's too late.* I have two responses to that thought. First, with God's help, it may *not* be too late. You still have time to share your perspectives and insights with your teenagers, even if they are older and seem to be moving out of your sphere of influence. If you feel you have made mistakes in the limits you have set, talk to them about that. They may be more understanding than you think. Second, it's never too late to start with other children you may have in your home. While this book deals specifically with issues important to adolescents, some of the issues have broader application to children of all ages. The chapters about church, television, and entertainment, for example, deal with issues that you face with your younger children as well as your teenagers.

I approach this topic with insight from personal experience in both my professional and family life. For nearly three decades, I worked with other people's kids. Thus, I have watched scores of parents struggle with very typical teenage conflicts, pressures, and decisions. During those years in youthwork, I offered counsel as a friend to parents of teenagers and as an objective outsider.

However, I am also the father of two daughters. I became much more personally involved with the teenage years as first our oldest daughter and then, four years later, our other daughter entered junior high school. I gained a great amount of empathy for other parents as my wife, Gail, and I endured our own struggles and agonized over our own tough choices.

But I do not want to presume that my experience should be normative, that all parents should relate to teenagers the way I do. In reality, each young person and each family is unique, with special characteristics, circumstances, and contingencies. So I have tried my best to look at the big picture, to check out the latest research, and to consult with many other parents and youth experts.

My goal is to give parents helpful information for making wise decisions in each of these critical areas. I want to provide positive motivation and practical answers. But I also want to give you *permission* to be a *strong parent,* exercising loving authority and making the tough choices that responsible parenting requires.

In a world where almost anything goes and where diversity and total tolerance are politically correct, parents can become paralyzed into inaction, intimidated by what other parents might think, or fearful of making mistakes. My prayer is that as you read this book, you will gain the courage to draw the line and to say no when you must. I pray that you will lovingly yet firmly guide your kids in the right direction.

Good parents have to be tenacious and make tough choices.

—Dave Veerman

CHAPTER 1

"Friends Are My Life!"

"Dave's not only my brother;
he's my best friend."
—Ricky Nelson to Harriet
from "Ricky, the Law Clerk"

THE SOFT FOOTSTEPS in the hall catching her attention, Barbara Murdock turns from the stove. "Where are you going, honey?" she calls out to her daughter.

"To The Deep End," answers fifteen-year-old Katie. "I'm meeting Shannon there."

"Come here. I need to talk with you for a minute," Barbara Murdock replies.

Katie turns and saunters back to the kitchen. Standing with hands on her hips, she scowls and says evenly, "OK, I'm here. Make it quick. I told Shannon I would be there at seven."

"Katie," begins her mom, "I know friends are important. Everyone needs friends. But you and Shannon have spent so much time together over the past few weeks, and when you're not together, you're talking on the phone." She pauses for a second to gather her thoughts and then continues. "And . . . well . . . it occurred to me that I really don't know her. I mean, what kind of girl is she?"

"Look, Mom," Katie replies tersely, "if this is going to be another rag-on-my-friends session, I don't want to hear it. Shannon's cool. She's my best friend, OK? So get off my case!"

Gathering her courage and raising her voice slightly, Barbara Murdock continues. "I'm sure that she's a wonderful girl, but, uh, we just don't know her. And, well, to be honest, I overheard some parents talking, and I thought I heard them say that a girl named Shannon had been getting into trouble at school. And, actually, I'm concerned for you. I just don't think you should hang around with the wrong kinds of kids."

"Oh, that's great!" answers Katie, angrily spitting out each word. "A few gossips spread lies, and you believe them. You don't believe me!" Suddenly she turns and walks back down the hall. Opening the door, she yells back, "Shannon is my friend. *She* believes me and believes in me. My friends treat me better than this stupid family does!" She slams the door and disappears into the night.

Upset and confused, Barbara Murdock looks out the kitchen window and watches Katie walk with determined steps down Oak Street in the direction of The Deep End, the new teen hangout located in the strip mall about a mile from the house. As she watches, she thinks, *Teenagers! Lord, help me!*

Arguments about friends aren't new in this house. Barbara and Dan Murdock engaged in similar conflicts with Katie's older brother, Bill, now nineteen. They watched with dismay as Bill's grades and interest in school slipped dramatically during his junior year after he had begun hanging around with Tony Crabel and the Butler boys. The Murdocks were sure that Bill had begun smoking back then, and that's when he started to get into trouble with his teachers. Since graduation, Bill has held a variety of jobs, and last fall he moved out and is living in an apartment on the other side of town. His life seems to be going nowhere. The Murdocks have begun to see the same tendencies in Katie, and they don't want a repeat performance. So the confrontations and arguments have begun.

The Challenge

Friends mean a great deal to teenagers. The intense need for friends begins in middle school with the rise of phone calls, notes, and cliques. At this stage early adolescents are developing their social skills. They are learning how to relate, communicate, and find their place in the social strata. During this time they become increasingly aware of the opposite sex, and suddenly relationships get complicated.

Peer Pull

Teenagers feel pulled into relationships for several reasons: survival, the need for independence, and the search for identity.

Survival. Many friendships are forged through survival. Early adolescents, for example, can feel lost in larger schools. Their peers can be very cruel to each other, shooting verbal insults like deadly arrows, spreading rumors, and ostracizing. So, like wagons in the Wild West, kids circle their friends for protection and security.

Independence. As teenagers move into high school, their need for friends takes on a different shape. They choose their friends not so much for survival as for companionship on the road to independence. Kids fifteen through eighteen years old are emerging adults; they are growing up and maturing, slower than they want, but often faster than their parents realize. These teens want to make their own decisions and find their own ways in the world. Although good parents want to help their teens become independent because they know that children eventually should leave home, parents sometimes become wary of the friends their teenagers choose. Parents know that the road from childhood to adulthood is filled with bumps and potholes. It's a tough transition. Along with getting a driver's license, choosing their own friends becomes an important symbol of independence. When parents question their teenagers about their relationships, they will often respond, "They are *my* friends!" emphasizing their personal choice of those friends.

Identity. Middle adolescents also feel pulled to friends as they share a common search for identity. High school kids are trying to discover who they are and where they fit in. As a result, they may try on a variety of personas and try out a number of groups. It's not that unusual to see a former cheer-leader mix with the tough crowd, a social butterfly turn to the burnouts, an athlete turn his or her attention to music, or a wallflower blossom as a member of the pom-pom squad. These dramatic swings involve changing friendships and can be very confusing to parents. But these changes reflect the teenagers' need to try on various identities, to see where they fit in. They want to be accepted and affirmed. They want to be loved. Parents may respond, "But *we* love them. Doesn't that count?" Yes, it does count. But parental love is not enough. Besides, teenagers figure that it's their parents' "job" to love them. Teenagers want to know if *anyone else* values them. In fact, some kids move from clique to clique as if they are asking, "Does anyone *out there* like me?"

When children are young, their playmates and closest friends usually live next door or down the street. Adolescents, however, tend to find their friends at school because their friendships are based much more on activities and interests. This change begins in junior high. Often the friendship shift can be difficult to understand and even painful for middle school students as they see their close friends move away from them and toward other interests and other groups. In high school, with an increasing number of sports, studies, and clubs, the shift continues and widens. High schools draw students from all over the commu-nity, so good friends may live on the other side of town. Once teenagers are old enough to drive, they find it relatively easy to spend time with friends who have similar ideas and interests and who give acceptance and affirmation. At this stage the pull of friendship reflects teenagers' growing awareness of themselves and their search for identity.

As teenagers push for independence and struggle to define

themselves, they may also try out different values. A young person who has grown up in a very conservative and safe environment may begin to make radical statements and take risks. This teen, for example, may endorse a social cause or may join a protest against a school policy or program. An introverted eighth grader may evolve into a party animal in high school. Or an adolescent who has been reared in a very strict home may try living on the wild side. This experimentation with values will influence friendships as teens move toward those kids who project a desired image or who endorse a specific lifestyle or cause. Values testing can be positive or negative. In either case, it tends to drive parents berserk as they try to figure out their adolescent children and understand what's going on inside them.

Peer Push

Once teenagers have responded to the pull of individual and group relationships, they feel a different force. The same friends that have pulled them into a group may then try to push them in directions they may not wish to go.

Much has been spoken and written about peer pressure because it is real and powerful. Peers influence people of all ages, even mature adults. Think of what influences you to buy a specific car model or to wear certain clothes. Even in casual discussions about everything from politics to sports, adults tend to choose their words carefully, depending on who is in the group. Most of the peer pressure that *adults* feel, however, is rather subtle; that is, usually no one tells us how to act or ridicules us for our fashion choices.

In contrast, adolescent peer pressure can be enormous and very obvious. Of course, some strong-willed, independent teens can set their own agenda and will lead the group rather than follow. But only a minority can withstand the pressure and do what is right despite the group. The majority of teenagers are influenced to some degree, and those with weak convictions and weak wills are very susceptible.

SUSCEPTIBILITY

Who's nurturing our kids? Parents? Schools? Churches? We know better. This is the first society in which young people are learning more from the media and their peer group than from previous generations. This makes them extremely susceptible to the latest fads—faddish ideas, behaviors, language—and also makes it hard for parents to pass on religious faith and practice.

—Quentin J. Schultze
author of *Redeeming Television*[1]

Because teenagers feel a strong need to fit in, they will do almost anything to be accepted by a preferred group and by their friends. Results of the pressure to conform appear first in hairstyles, fashions, and musical tastes. Teenagers may even develop characteristic ways of walking and talking. These changes can be positive or negative, depending on the circle of friends and the amount of pressure.

All parents hope their teenagers will connect with *good* kids who will help their teens become better people. Sometimes that actually happens. I know several girls who decided to try out for the junior high volleyball team *together*. My friend's son would not have thought twice about auditioning for the play, until his best friend did. And I have seen students in strong youth ministries encourage their friends to live for Christ and then hold them accountable.

Too often, however, the negative influences prevail, and some of the results can be deadly. Most kids who smoke, drink, and use illegal drugs began those destructive habits through the urging of a friend or group of friends. Peer pressure can also lead to reckless driving, vandalism, stealing, sexual abuse, and other crimes. And we hear terrible stories of young people dying as a result of macho acts or taking various dares.

A young person's choice of friends, therefore, is crucial.

The Conflict

Teenagers' need for friends has a direct impact on the family. As teenagers grow older, they spend less and less time with the family, preferring instead to be with their peers. At a time when parents want to have some influence on their teenagers' decisions and choices, their teens are pushing them away. It becomes hard, then, for parents to know the people with whom their teens are spending time. Like Barbara Murdock, parents may have very little information about their teenagers' friends.

Parents can respond to their teenagers' choices in friends in several ways. Three responses are especially *counterproductive:* passivity, confrontation, and resignation.

Naive Passivity

Some parents actually see no problem with any of their teenagers' associates, even friends with obvious character flaws. It's as if these parents wear blinders or rose-colored glasses. Then they are shocked when their kids get into trouble. They typically respond, "Not my Craig!" or "Suzie would never do such a thing!" Neighbors, friends, and even relatives have seen the teenager slide in the wrong direction, but the parents were clueless. Perhaps Craig and Suzie have learned how to fool their parents, acting one way at home and another way everywhere else. Or perhaps the parents are choosing to overlook or rationalize away the clues and symptoms: the clothes smell of smoke because the kids had to sit in the smoking area of the restaurant; the grades have been slipping because the teachers aren't fair; the rash of curfew violations occurred because of car trouble; the report of seeing the family automobile at a local lovers' lane must have been mistaken; the slurred speech was caused by lack of sleep.

These naive parents really believe that their children are strong-willed enough to resist all peer pressure. They think that if friends are less than desirable, the son or daughter will be willing and able to pull them up. These moms and dads make few demands on their teenagers, have few rules, and ask for very little information about their kids' friends or activities.

This approach can lead to disaster. All children, especially

PULLED UP OR PULLED DOWN?

If I could put a hidden microphone on your teenager's best friend for one day, I would be able to tell a lot about your child. If the best friends cheat on tests, your son or daughter probably does also. The same goes with lying, showing disrespect, using drugs, and so forth.

Show me *your* friends, and I'll show you a lot about *you*.

Raising the morals of two or three friends is nearly impossible for your teenager. To illustrate this, have your son or daughter stand on a chair (representing his or her higher morals and standards than the friends' standards). Then have the teenager try to pull two people up to the higher level. It can't be done. In fact, the opposite usually will occur—the group almost always pulls the individual down to their level.

A tree is known by its fruit. Watch your teenager's friends and you are looking at what your child will become in a very short time.

—Bill Sanders
youth speaker, author, and
television host of *Straight Talk*

early adolescents, need rules, controls, and guidance. Left to themselves, they can self-destruct. Even high school students need parental involvement; love means being in touch, getting involved, being concerned with teenagers. Many young people *are* good kids and have the strength and courage to resist peer pressure. But many adolescents are weak, and nearly all are susceptible to peer pressure. For parents to assume that their teenagers are different from the norm and would *never* make a mistake or get into trouble would be foolish indeed. Pretending that everything is rosy won't make it so.

Angry Confrontation

Another common reaction to the friends issue is for parents to confront their teenagers directly about their involvement with the "wrong kinds of kids." This can be the opposite of the naive passivity response. In this case, parents assume that the friends are bad and are engaged in all sorts of questionable behavior. They attack the teenager, questioning, accusing, judging, and perhaps even calling names ("About your friend Kenny. I don't want you hanging around with him. He looks as if he is on drugs, a real burnout! For all I know, you are probably on drugs too!").

Besides leading to the inevitable shouting match, complete with hateful words, name calling, threats, and slamming doors, this approach builds a huge barrier to effective communication, with the teenager withdrawing and keeping his or her thoughts, plans, dreams, and relationships secret. And if parents are wrong about the values of the friends, the quality of the friendship, or the behavior of the child, the outburst could severely damage the parent-child relationship. Then, when the teenager exclaims, "You never trust me!" he or she would be right.

Even when the friends are less than desirable and parents are correct in their assessment, loud confrontation is still a mistake. It is a wrong approach, first, because it moves the focus from the problem to the parents and their out-of-control response. I learned this several years ago in my work with young teenagers. If I calmly and firmly explained and enforced the rules, most of the kids would listen and obey. Even troublemakers whom I had to punish by removing them from the room understood what I had done and why. They didn't like my decision, but they knew that I was doing what I was supposed to do. My words and actions were directed at their behavior and not against them personally. In contrast, whenever I yelled, belittled, or called names, the kids, the objects of my displeasure, *always* turned against me. I have also seen this when I have lost my temper with one of our daughters. My angry and loud attack would always escalate the conflict rather than move it toward resolution. My response had made me part of the problem.

Angry confrontation is also wrong because it blocks communication. As mentioned above, one of the main lessons that teenagers learn from shouting matches is to keep their actions and thoughts secret. Often the issue boils down to *power* and *control.* Young people know that they have only limited power at home but nearly unlimited control of their thoughts and actions away from home. When they realize that they may be blasted for telling their parents about friends and activities, they will decide to remain silent, figuring that they can't get into trouble for what their parents *don't* know.

Finally, the loud confrontation approach is counterproductive because it erodes self-esteem and may push teenagers *toward* the wrong friends, the opposite of the desired direction. After an intense discussion about a specific relationship, the teen may feel sure that the friend in question is the only person who really

I FORBID YOU!

One common response to a negative relationship is to forbid the teenager from seeing that friend. If the friends don't see each other, these parents reason, then they'll stop being friends. However, this approach is unwise for several reasons.

First, it's unenforceable. There's virtually no way you can enforce the quarantine, particularly if the kids go to the same school. Will you go to school every day with your teenager, walk the halls, sit at lunch and in class? Your teenager would run away from home at that prospect.

Second, kids won't obey it. A major national study revealed that fewer than 10 percent of sixteen-year-olds would stop seeing a friend at their parents' insistence. Younger children may. But the older your kids become, the less successful you'll be when you "lay down the law."

Third, it slams the doors of communication. Keeping communication open is vital. By shutting off communication with a single-sentence command, you risk damaging your long-term relationship with your teenager.

Finally, it short-circuits potential growth. Making a decision like this cuts off your teenager's opportunity to develop decision-making skills.

—Len Kageler
*Helping Your Teenager
Cope with Peer Pressure*[2]

knows and accepts him or her. If kids don't feel understood and loved at home, they will go elsewhere to meet those needs, and they will usually go to their peers. They will find comfort from the peer group that affirms them, makes them feel wanted, and doesn't criticize every move. Some friends may even feel sorry for the teenager whose parents have reacted negatively. The friends will side with the teenager as the poor, misunderstood victim of the tirade. Other teenagers may become so convinced of what they have said in their verbal defense of a friend that they build up that friend in their minds and become even more committed to the friendship. Or when hit with an angry blast, some teenagers may react out of spite and do exactly the opposite of what their parents want, just to get even ("I'll show them!").

Very seldom does angry confrontation help solve a problem, especially in relationships. Kids need parents who love enough to be firm but who are mature and controlled enough to keep their cool.

Tired Resignation

Some parents become battle weary and just give in. During the early adolescent years, these parents tried hard to protect their teenagers from all negative outside influences. But gradually they wore down and became disgusted with the whole process. Eventually their attitude became, "Let the kids do what they want." Although the parents may not be conscious of this attitude and they probably wouldn't verbalize it, they have given up. Thus, when their son or daughter gets a driver's license, the parents' approach seems to be "out of sight, out of mind." If they don't know about a problem, they won't have to deal with it.

I have witnessed this phenomenon in a wide variety of families. When their kids were approaching adolescence, these parents, virtually without exception, were scared to death and began to seek advice, resources, and answers. They were concerned about music, movies, videos, language, habits, attitudes, and friends. Repeatedly, however, I have seen those same parents *stop* looking for help when their kids were in high school and were struggling with much more difficult and important issues.

The result for these families with tired and resigned parents is disaster. Kids need patient parents who will stay involved with them over the long haul, even when the going gets difficult.

So, What's a Parent to Do?

What are the choices we face as our teenagers choose friends? We can adopt the ostrich mentality and put our head in the sand, hoping our kids will choose the right friends; if they don't, we can just hope that their friends will not be a bad influence on them. We can become alarmed at our teenagers' choice of friends and confront them about it, hoping that they will see our perspective and choose different friends. We can give up and hope they will turn out well in the end.

I'm sure you will agree that none of these alternatives is satisfactory. But what are our other choices? I see several alternatives. But I must warn you that these choices are not easy. They will require our energy, commitment, and patience.

The Choice

While you can't choose your teenagers' friends for them, you can prepare yourself and them for making good choices, and you can take the initiative in creating an atmosphere in which they can develop healthy friendships.

Prepare

As you watch your teenagers grow older, keep in mind that you will not like every friend they choose. Conflicts seem inevitable because whatever you say about a friend may be interpreted as a threat and taken personally. So you need to be careful in how you react. Before you respond to a specific child and a specific situation, here is what you can do to prepare for the potential stress and conflicts.

Pray. All Christian parents would agree on the importance of prayer, yet often we forget to pray for our children, especially regarding their self-esteem and their friendships. When our daughter Kara was in first grade, she and Gail would regularly pray together that a family *with a child Kara's age* would move into the vacant house down the street. It happened, and Michelle became Kara's favorite playmate and closest friend. Gail is much more sensitive to relationship issues than I, so she has repeated that process in our current neighborhood. Over the years, she has prayed—for our girls and with them—that they would find good, Christian friends.

One day last year our younger daughter, Dana (then a sophomore in high school), came home from school excited about a new friendship. "She's a Christian, Dad. I've been asking God for a Christian friend in high school, and he led me to Lisa."

Pray daily about your children's friendships; start when they are young. It's an important issue.

Observe. Be aware of what is going on in your kids' lives. This should begin long before adolescence. Understand how they are developing mentally, physically, spiritually, emotionally, and *socially.* Books, magazines, doctors, and other parents are excellent sources of helpful information and counsel. You will find it much easier to guide your teenagers if you know what is going on in their lives. If your seventh-grade son seems to be gravitating toward questionable relationships, you should consider the reasons for that move and begin to steer him in a better direction. As mentioned above, unobservant parents are surprised when "suddenly" a son or daughter hangs around with the wrong kids. In reality, the change in direction probably was gradual and steady and should have been seen months before the crisis. If you become a student of each child, then changes and growth won't catch you off guard.

Set limits. Children of all ages need rules, limits to their behavior. Responsible parents set those limits and enforce them. As children grow and mature, the rules change, and they are given more freedom and choices. If you have developed in your home a climate in which realistic rules are discussed, set, and enforced, your teenagers won't be surprised that they have rules. They may push against the limits and argue with you, but they will understand the importance of having rules.

Talk. Get into the habit of talking positively with your kids about their friends. In other words, don't cross-examine them, look for problems, and criticize. Ask questions that demonstrate your concern for the friends and your desire to understand them and get to know them.

- "How's Gretchen's mom doing? You told me that she wasn't feeling well. Let's pray for her."
- "Jake seems really nice. What activities is he involved in at school?"
- "Hey, your birthday's coming up in just six weeks. What kind of party do you want, and whom do you want to invite?"
- "I was sorry to hear that Linda's parents have separated. How have you been able to help Linda through all of this?"

There's no guarantee, of course, that your teenagers will talk with you about *all* their relationship issues, but talking positively about their friends will greatly improve the chances. If you talk about friends only when trouble arises, your teens won't want to talk about them at all.

Take the Initiative

Besides preparing for your teenagers' friendships by setting a climate in your home, you need to take action. You can do several things to take the initiative to head off problem friendships.

Stay Involved. Stay involved in your teenagers' lives through the junior high and high school years. Work on parent committees, sell refreshments at athletic contests, and chaperone special activities and trips. This will familiarize you with your teenagers' world, and you will see their friends *on their turf.*

Also, work hard at staying involved one-on-one with your teenagers. In other words, communicate! To that suggestion many parents would respond: "That's easy to say, but our daughter just won't talk to me. And when she does, it's with grunts or one-word answers." I didn't say it would be easy; remember, these are *tough* choices. Actually, if your teenagers don't talk much with you, relax—they are normal. Their lives are

---

MEETING NEEDS

We make friends with people who meet a need in our lives. If Gloria doesn't feel love at home, she'll likely look elsewhere. If Cecil is short and feels intimidated, he may befriend a star athlete. And if Dola is shy, she may be attracted to Bert, who's the definition of gregarious.

There's nothing necessarily wrong with choosing friends who meet particular needs. God didn't create us to be self-fulfilled: He created us to be in fellowship and friendship with other people. Moreover, families can't meet all the needs teenagers have.

At the same time, if our teenagers turn to negative friendships to meet their needs, we need to consider what's attractive about those friendships. What need do they fulfill? When we understand the needs, we discover appropriate ways to respond to the negative situations we see developing.

—Len Kageler
Helping Your Teenager Cope with Peer Pressure[3]

changing in every area, including their relationship to you. As children grow through adolescence, they should be moving toward more of a peer relationship with us. Don't misunderstand; we will always be their parents. But eventually we should be able to relate to our children as *adults*. During this transition time, relationships with older adolescents may be quite awkward. Talking with your teenager will take *work*.

Listening. The mark of a good communicator is the ability to focus on a person and really listen to what he or she is saying. When your teenagers talk, listen carefully; don't interrupt or let your mind wander.

Timing. Often we parents want to talk with our children when *we* are ready. If you are serious about communication, however, you should be patient and wait to talk when *your teenagers* want to talk.

Creativity. Sometimes it helps to create opportunities for talk, for teachable moments, so use your imagination. For example, you could schedule regular breakfast "appointments" during which you and your teenagers eat at a restaurant together before school once a week. Or you could ask your teens to play a favorite CD for you and then explain the words and music to you. Or you could make a *family expression board* on which each member of the family can post thoughts, verses, cartoons, or whatever for everyone to read. Or you could have a question envelope into which family members are encouraged to put any question they would like the whole family to discuss over dinner. Put your imagination in gear and think of what you could do or say to get conversation rolling. For more ideas for discussion starters with your teenagers, see *Getting Your Kid to Talk,* listed in the resources section at the end of this book.

My point is simply that you should use creativity, take the

initiative, and work hard at communicating with your teenagers. Stay involved in their lives.

Provide Opportunities. Many parents bemoan the sad state of their adolescents' relationships, but they don't give them any opportunities to meet the right kinds of kids. Explore options that will possibly place your teenagers with people who share their values. The church youth group is an obvious place to start. But beyond that, many student ministries may offer your teenagers a place to belong and find friends. Chapter 3 will discuss the importance of supporting student ministries like Campus Life, Young Life, Fellowship of Christian Athletes, Student Venture, Christian camps, and so forth. While I can't guarantee that your son or daughter will meet the right kinds of kids and establish positive friendships at those meetings and activities, I do know that they have a far better chance there than at school or in the neighborhood. Some of our daughters' closest friends live and go to schools on the opposite end of town. Kara and

ATTRACT YOUR TEENS' FRIENDS

You cannot choose your teens' friends, but you can influence those friends when they are in your home. So the big question is: How do you get them over to your house and keep them there as much as possible?

Make your home a place of acceptance and laughter. Demonstrate warmth and authenticity. You don't have to be "hip" or "cool" (in fact, don't try to be!), but you do have to be real.

My parents helped me build a lighted basketball court when I was twelve years old, and for all the years of my adolescence, our driveway was the neighborhood hangout. Now that I think about it, their bedroom window was right next to the court!

—Len Woods
Minister to Students,
Christ Community Church,
Ruston, Louisiana

Dana met these friends in our church's youth group, and they solidified their friendships at summer camp.

Also, you can provide other opportunities for good friendships by planning outings with families who have kids the same age as yours. Invite a family over to dinner, have a picnic with a few families, go camping together, or go to a ball game together.

The goal here is to expose your teenagers to potential positive friendships. Create opportunities for them to meet other good kids.

Reach Out. Taking the initiative to reach out will take work, but it will be worth it. Get to know your children's friends. The easiest way to do this is to make your home adolescent-friendly. This includes stocking the refrigerator and pantry with soft drinks and snack foods, providing a place for them to watch television, play games, fool around with the computer, and listen to music, and generally being relaxed about your furniture and carpet. In short, it means making your home a place where your kids would want to bring their friends. When the friends do come over, show sincere interest in each one and treat them with respect. The results will be worth your investment of money and time.

Until teenagers receive the coveted driver's license, their parents have to play chauffeur and drive all over town to athletic practices, music lessons, school events, friends' homes, etc. Instead of treating this as a painful chore, see it as an opportunity to spend time with your teenagers and their friends. And when you drive your adolescents to a new friend's house, take a few minutes to go inside and meet the friend's parents. This in-home visit will tell you much about the friend and will open the communication lines with the friend's parents. Then, when your teen says, "Why can't I? Tina's mom lets her!" you can call Tina's parents and talk with them about the decision because you have met them.

FRIENDS FEAR

The best protection you can give your teenagers against choosing the wrong kinds of friends is to give your kids such a high view of themselves that they will be unlikely to choose friends who are far below their level of self-worth. Most kids tend to choose their friends from the social strata where they themselves feel most comfortable. If teenagers have a high view of themselves, they will be less likely to choose friends who will drag them down to a lower level. On the other hand, if teenagers suffer from low self-esteem or feel like a reject, they will tend to choose friends who also feel like rejects.

But sometimes kids experiment with their choices of friends. They aren't sure exactly where they fit, so they try on a variety of friendships for size. It's always good to allow teenagers the opportunity to choose their own friends and then to accept those choices as far as it is possible.

—Wayne Rice
speaker, author, and cofounder
of Youth Specialties

Give yourself time to get to know your teenagers' friends. Many parents have discovered that if they are patient, they will discover the good things their teenagers like about their friends. Parents lose a lot of credibility with their children when they denounce their friends without knowing them.

Reach out to your kids' friends. It's a tough choice but an important one.

Affirm Your Child. One of the primary internal tasks children work on in their adolescent years is forming their identity. They struggle to know who they really are, what they can do, and where they fit in. Usually parents can tell a lot about their teenagers by their friends. Kids who don't think very highly of themselves will tend to make friends at the same level or below. The implication for parents should be obvious: We should work hard at developing their self-esteem.

Let your teenagers know that God created them as special people with unique talents, gifts, and abilities. Let your teens know that you love and highly value them. Let them know that they are *good*. Try to catch your adolescents doing something *right;* then praise them for it. (Too often they hear from us only when they mess up or disobey.) Offer your praise with no "buts" (". . . *but* you should have kept your eye on the second baseman in the third inning" or ". . . *but* you may have been a little flat on that high G" or ". . . *but* I wish you would act like that all the time"). Instead, offer your affirmation with no strings attached and no hidden agenda.

Of course, true affirmation takes more than saying it. Words are important, but talk is cheap. Your children will know that you value them when you make the effort to attend their recitals, games, open houses, contests, and concerts, when you nurse them back to health, or when you work with them on a difficult class project. In other words, they need *you* more than anything else.

If your teens know that you love and appreciate them, they won't be so quick to look for acceptance and affirmation from friends.

Guide toward Independence. As we discussed earlier, adolescents are moving toward independence. They want to make their own decisions and choices. Often the area in which they declare their independence is friendship; in other words, they want to choose their friends. This issue is magnified if these teens have few opportunities to make important decisions. In fact, when reined in by overly protective parents, some teenagers react defiantly and will even sneak out to be with the kids whom *they* have chosen as friends. And the more their parents dislike a specific individual or group, the more the teens will move in that direction.

You need to help your kids mature and grow up and away

from you. That's the job of responsible parents. So look for ways to allow your teenagers to make choices and decisions. With a driver's license comes added responsibility and freedom. Don't suddenly allow these new drivers to drive wherever and whenever they want. That would be foolish. On the other hand, look for opportunities to allow your teenagers to take the car. Gradually increase the freedom as your teens show maturity and respect for your regulations and limits.

Do the same in other areas, such as money management. You may choose to give your teenagers their budgeted clothing allowance and allow them to buy their own clothes. (We will discuss money and spending in chapter 8.) Reinforce this lesson with Jesus' story of the loaned money as recorded in Matthew 25:14-30. In this story, the master tells his responsible employees, "Well done, good and faithful servant! You have been faithful with a few things; I will put you in charge of many things. Come and share your master's happiness!" (Matthew 25:21). Look for other ways to give your teenagers freedom and responsibility for "many things," as they prove to be faithful in the "few things."

Another important way to help kids gain independence the right way is negotiation. You may have a situation in which you want your child to break off all contact with a certain friend. Instead of making that demand, however, talk it out and try to reach a compromise. In every successful negotiation, both parties understand that they have to give in a bit, to move away from their original position. So you may have to allow some contact in exchange for your son or daughter spending time with other kids too. Or you may both agree to have the friend over for dinner. The operative principle here is that parents should try to *guide* their teenagers, not *block* them. Discussing, providing alternatives and other options, and negotiating are ways to guide. Negotiation says to your teenagers that you see them as adults, not as young children.

Adolescents who feel trusted and respected at home are less likely to rebel and much less likely to gravitate toward kids whose values and lifestyles differ from the family's.

Confront in Love. In even the best homes, teenagers will push the limits and test their parents' resolve. And remember, teens are still kids; they will act their age and make adolescent mistakes. At some point you may find that your teenagers will hang around with the wrong group. That's when you must have a serious talk with them. A good relationship will help ease the tension of the moment. But you still may have angry or frustrated teens on your hands.

Confront your teenagers with the situation as you see it, slowly and calmly explaining your concerns. Counsel them about the possible pitfalls. Listen carefully to their answers, then propose a solution. Try to talk it through and negotiate. If your teens react angrily and don't want to listen, firmly hold the line. Exercise your strong will and outline your expectations and the penalties for disobedience. You are the parent; that's your responsibility.

CROWD CONTROL

When I was fourteen, I ran with the wrong crowd. I knew my parents were not happy with my friends, but at that point I didn't care. I resented their opinions. They wisely chose not to yell at me and berate my friends, but they let me know that they were concerned with the direction I was headed. They didn't nag, but they also didn't lower their expectations of what they expected from me. And I knew they were praying for me. They welcomed my friends into our home and treated them with respect. That impressed me. Eventually I saw the negative effect of the friends I had chosen. I'm glad my parents kept their standards high.

—Karen, eighteen-year-old high school student

Help Other Parents. I have been in youth ministry virtually all of my adult life. Like many people, I used to think that eventually I would become too old for youthwork. I assumed that I would reach a point when I wouldn't understand kids anymore and when they wouldn't listen to me because of my age. I have found, however, that age has not made that much difference. In fact, most adolescents relate well to certain adults of almost any age: an understanding aunt or grandparent, a caring coach, an empathetic teacher, a listening counselor, a loving pastor. Concern, understanding, and love can bridge almost any generation gap.

I also know, however, that being a parent handicaps me, at times, in relating to my own teenagers. They harbor secrets that they won't share with me. They have questions that they won't ask me. They struggle with doubts and dreams about which they won't ask my help. Perhaps they don't want to worry me, disappoint me, or anger me. Perhaps they are afraid that I will judge them quickly and won't take time to hear them out. Or perhaps they really do think that I am "over the hill" and don't understand kids their age.

That's reality. But that's precisely why I want other caring Christian adults to love our daughters. And that's why I continue to be an adult friend to other parents' kids—at church, in the neighborhood, and at school.

My challenge is simply this: look for ways to help other parents with their teenagers. You can do this by helping with the youth ministry, by offering to listen if they need someone to talk to, and by affirming kids by your words and actions (giving compliments, sending notes, clipping newspaper articles with their names and pictures, etc.). And while you're doing this, share with other parents your burden for your own teenagers. Ask them to pray for you and to be a friend to your kids too.

When we care for each other's kids, we truly share each other's burdens and "fulfill the law of Christ" (Galatians 6:2). That's the body of Christ in action (see 1 Corinthians 12:12–13:13).

* * *

The issue of friends looms large with teenagers. As teenagers learn about themselves and how to socialize, they find their friends are important mirrors for the changes going on in their lives. Friends are a source of encouragement, security, and growth. Parents should enter this important area with care and concern. Rather than naively assuming that everything will be all right, loudly confronting teens with their demands, or giving up, parents should stay involved with their teenagers, provide opportunities for them to find good friends, reach out to their friends, affirm them, guide them toward independence, confront them in love when necessary, and help other parents.

THINK IT THROUGH
1. Who are your teenagers' best friends?
2. In what ways are those friends a positive influence on your teenagers?
3. How are those friends a negative influence?
4. When did you last affirm your teenagers' friends?
5. What are you doing to keep the communication channels open with your kids?
6. What will you do to promote your teens' self-esteem?
7. What choices can you allow your teenagers to make to guide them toward independence?
8. How will you help your adolescents find good friends?
9. What will be your strategy if you have to confront your teenager about a friendship or group of friends?
10. What can you do to help other parents of teenagers in your church or neighborhood?

CHAPTER 2

"I Need a Date to Homecoming"

"The trouble with you guys is your dates are too involved these days. . . . When I used to go on a date with a girl, I'd just go over to her house, play some records, or take her for a walk— something like that."
—Ozzie to David and Ricky from "The Date"

"MONICA!" FRANK GREGORY calls up the stairs to his daughter. "Telephone! It's a boy!"

"Oh, Dad! Be quiet. He'll *hear* you!" replies Monica, emerging from the bathroom, obviously annoyed by her father's comment. She quickly picks up the phone in her room and slowly shuts the door as she begins to speak.

"Hello . . . Nick? Sure, I remember you. You're a sophomore from the high school, right. . . ?" is all her dad can hear as the door closes behind Monica.

Frank Gregory walks back to the family room. "Well, Janet, it's another boy. This time a high school guy. I think she said *Nick*. Do we know any Nick?"

Janet Gregory shakes her head. "No, I don't think so. Frank, I think that's the third boy this week! Maybe he will ask her to homecoming. She will be on cloud nine if she gets to go to the high school homecoming. Our little girl is becoming a woman. Isn't it exciting?"

"I suppose," replies Frank, "but don't you think she's a little young to be dating? I mean, she's only fourteen."

"Yes, but Monica is mature for her age. I think she can handle it," replies Janet. "Anyway, Joan Bennett's daughter, Christine, is dating, and she's a year younger than Monica. These are the nineties. Things are different from when we were their age!"

Frank shrugs and sighs. "I guess you're right. Maybe I have these feelings because Monica is our oldest. But she sure is growing up fast."

* * *

Although Monica is only in eighth grade, she has been dating for a month. Every night she fields calls from boys or from her girlfriends talking about boys. Usually her classmates call her, but high school guys ask her out too.

Like most parents, Frank and Janet Gregory don't know how to handle their daughter's sudden interest in the opposite sex. Just a couple of years ago, Monica thought boys were jerks, or at best they were tolerable. Lately, however, boys are the only topic of her conversations. Frank and Janet are confused. What should they do?

The Challenge

Make no mistake, the pressure to pair up is real, even on kids who have no interest in the opposite sex. Until seventh grade or so, most children stick with kids their own age and sex. I live next door to an elementary school; daily I observe kids walking to and from school and playing during recess. Seldom, if ever, have I seen boys and girls together unless they are playing keep-away, throwing snowballs, or chasing each other. I'm sure there are exceptions to this rule, and kids may tease one another about "liking" someone. Overall, however, they have no romantic or sexual interest.

That's natural, of course, and the way it should be. Most children of that age haven't begun puberty, and the appropriate hormones haven't kicked in. And they certainly aren't ready emotionally for serious boy-girl relationships.

So if they aren't attracted naturally, what is the source of the pressure? Adults. In many ways, the pressure comes from the adult world. Through the media and even through the structure of school events, adult society pushes kids to pair up.

Media Pressure

Check out the television shows, magazines, movies, and books. They feature stories about dating, romance, and even sex. Perhaps the writers and television producers think the stories are cute, or maybe they are just unaware of the differences between adults and children and of the developmental issues involved. (A cynical view would say that they don't care and just want to make money.) Whatever the reason, adults continue to imply, suggest, and even insist that children take an interest in the opposite sex. Need proof? Here are just a few quick examples from my recent experience. I'm sure you can find many others if you look.

Many television programs targeted to children, especially weekly sitcoms, feature children or early adolescents in starring roles. Often the story lines for these shows involve complications in boy-girl relationships for the young characters. In some shows, such as *Blossom,* the lead character grows up before our eyes and has to deal with many opposite-sex entanglements. In an episode of *My So-Called Life,* a junior high school boy was set up with a blind date, and he double-dated with a high school friend. Tune in any show with kid stars, and you'll soon see a main story or subplot involving opposite-sex intrigues.

On Tuesdays, the *Chicago Tribune* includes a section entitled "KidNews." Glancing at the latest edition, I can see that the target audience is kids from age seven to fourteen. The "What's the Word" column has short book reviews by kids ages seven, nine, eleven, and thirteen. The "Ask Anything" column has letters from kids eleven and thirteen. (The thirteen-year-old wrote, "I like this guy. I was thinking that I should change to make him interested in me. What do I do?" She signed the letter "Hopelessly in Love.") "Backtalk" features letters to the editor from kids eleven through fourteen. In another column, kids from age eleven to thirteen review movies. Although the readers are very young, many articles and stories feature boy-girl relationships. Published at the beginning of February, this particular issue highlighted

Valentine's Day. One column has candy hearts strung across the top with the following sayings, one on each piece of candy: "Dear," "Soul Mate," "Let's Kiss," "I Will," and "Come On." The subtitle highlights the thrust of the topic: "Are you someone's secret admirer? Let your true love know you care." The following excerpt from a book review captures the essence of the whole issue: "Get in the mood for Valentine's Day with the new series Love Stories. . . . In *My First Love* by Callie West, Amy Wyse feels pressure to get good grades and still spend lots of time with her first boyfriend, Chris. *Sharing Sam,* by Katherine Applegate, is more melodramatic: Allison and her dying friend, Isabella, both fall in love with the same guy. There's nothing like a good love story when you're in the mood." Evidently the editors of this *Chicago Tribune* insert think kids as young as seven need advice about dating.

SITCOMS—THE NEXT GENERATION

Many television situation comedies feature adolescents and have stories that relate to typical teenage conflicts; thus, their target audience is high school and junior high students. When these programs go into syndication, however, the audience moves down a level; that is, younger children. . . . [who] are fed a steady diet of older adolescent issues and information, contributing to their loss of childhood.
—Jack Crabtree, executive director of Long Island Campus Life

But let's face it; those television examples and the excerpts from "KidNews" are pretty innocuous. They don't promote promiscuity or rebellion. So what's the big deal? The big deal is the subtle implication that love and dating are normal for this age group. Instead of letting kids be kids, adults push them to act older.

School Pressure

Schools can also contribute to the pressure to date. For example, many junior high schools sponsor dances. Kids can come alone, but dances usually involve choosing an opposite-sex partner with whom to dance. Other schools have activity nights that provide a variety of activities that may include a dance.

Our neighborhood middle school sponsors monthly activity nights. When each of our daughters attended that school, I took my turn as a parent chaperone for these all-school events. Over the years, my various responsibilities included serving refreshments, organizing floor hockey, supervising volleyball, and other chaperone-type tasks. One Friday night I was stationed in a hall at the foot of a stairway that led to a second-floor gymnasium. My job was to keep an eye on the hall and stairs, making sure that kids didn't do anything weird—an easy and boring responsibility. As I stood and watched from my end-of-the-hall observation post, I noticed that most of the sixth graders, especially the boys, would go upstairs to the gym to play basketball or volleyball or to the wrestling room to play floor hockey. Most of the eighth graders, however, would hang around in the dimly lit commons area, looking cool, listening to the records, and dancing occasionally. Both the sixth graders and the eighth graders seemed to know where they fit in. The seventh graders, however, were different and were the most fascinating group to watch. They seemed to spend much of their time running up and down the stairs, between the gym and the dance. Filled with ambivalence, they didn't know where they fit in or where to go. They thought they should be older and be at the dance, but they really wanted to shoot baskets.

In all of my work with early adolescents, I have found that just a few of them, usually the older ones, are even interested in the opposite sex. Even in our on-campus ministry meetings with public school kids, Sunday school classes, and church youth group meetings, the crowd would segregate themselves by gender. I must add that both of our daughters (now nineteen and sixteen) acquired an interest in boys during seventh or eighth grade and would talk about who was "going out" with whom. Obviously our daughters were growing physically, emotionally, and socially. During this time, they began to spend more time in the bathroom, fixing their hair, checking their clothes, and searching for blemishes. Their interest in boys was intriguing, exciting, and fun, but they certainly were not ready to date. Yet that's what they felt pressured to do at every activity night.

The pressure intensifies as kids enter high school. High school freshmen may be as young as fourteen years old, yet they are almost expected to date. In many schools, the first big event of the school year is homecoming. Besides the class competition, the queen and her court, and the big game, the homecoming dance looms large on the horizon during the very first weeks of school. In some schools, this dance is a formal occasion, almost as big as the prom. Girls are thrilled to be asked, and they make plans with their dates and friends for dinner and after-dance activities. Many who aren't asked to homecoming feel lonely and rejected.

Again, on the surface, junior high and senior high dances are no big deal. Certainly they aren't passion pits or sin centers that Christian parents need to fear and fight. As with the "KidNews" articles, the problem is more subtle; it's the pressure to pair up, the unspoken message that dating at a young age is normal, common, and expected.

Fourteen-year-old Colleen is attractive and physically mature for her age. Fresh from junior high and having to deal daily with the antics of seventh- and eighth-grade boys, Colleen enjoys the sudden interest shown by "much more mature" sophomores and juniors. They stop to talk with her in the hall. Some of them flirt with her, and a few call her at night. And, get this, a senior guy asked her to homecoming! What should Colleen do? Even if her parents have insisted that she not date until later, they will feel the pressure of this situation.

Peer Pressure

In addition to feeling pressure from the adult world, kids also feel pressure from their peers. In fact, the peer pressure in the past decade has resulted in some interesting shifts in the meaning of dating language. Junior high school kids in the area in which our family lives often announce that they are "going out" with or are "going steady" with so-and-so. Several decades ago, when you and I were dating, *going out* meant that we were dating one-on-one, and *going steady* meant that we had entered an exclusive dating relationship with one person. However, today, at least in our area, "going out" with someone may mean that you talk to each other in the halls, that you call each other on the phone, that you are officially interested in each other, and that you are romantically attracted to each other. You may never actually go out on a date. "Going steady" can be anything from having a "special" relationship for a few weeks to having an exclusive dating relationship for several months or years. For the purposes of this book, I will use the term *dating* to mean going out in a one-on-one relationship.

People who are already dating inadvertently and sometimes intentionally put pressure on teenagers who are not dating. The dating teens talk about their latest romantic interests and what they did last weekend, implying that the nondating teen is missing great fun. All of this heightens the interest and adds to the pressure to date.

The Conflict

Interest in the opposite sex and all the dating talk can be very confusing to parents. On the one hand, they want their children to remain young and innocent. Going out on a date is an obvious sign that a child is growing up. On the emotional level, parents would like to forbid their kids from dating—forever!

On the other hand, these parents also feel the pressure from society and their children. When their kids say, "Everybody's doing it," parents begin to wonder and to doubt their resolve. And when their kids give specific examples ("Tom's parents say it's fine" or "Katie gets to go, and her dad is a minister"), the doubts intensify. This becomes especially tough when the focus falls on a specific event or party, such as the homecoming dance or prom, where *"everyone* else is going!"

Also remember that parents are subjected to and influenced by the television sitcoms, movies, and other media messages. Whether or not they buy into the prevailing cultural philosophy and societal standards, parents can't help but be intimidated by them. This is a real struggle for parents who are trying their best to be responsible and to raise their kids the right way.

Extroverted moms and dads may fear that their sons or daughters could become social misfits; they certainly don't want that! When they hear of parties and proms and plans, they hint that their children should get involved. And when friends' kids are dating and theirs aren't, these parents worry and can become almost frantic.

In addition, many parents remember their early romantic

interests and dating attempts and may use their experience to rationalize their kids' early involvement with the opposite sex.

- Simone and Jerry started dating in junior high school. Their relationship continued through high school, and a couple of years after graduation, they got married. They have enjoyed a good marriage over the years. Using their relationship as an example, they don't see any problem with kids dating in junior high.
- "Nonexistent" describes Betsy's high school dating experience. Boys just didn't show any interest in her. Eventually she met Carl at work. After they dated for a few months, they got married and had a couple of children. But the marriage didn't work, so Betsy is a single mom. When her seventh-grade daughter, Carla, reported that a sixteen-year-old neighbor had asked her out, Betsy was excited. She believes and hopes that Carla's experience will be different from her own.
- Girls have been calling Alan almost every night. Word is that they think he's "hot." Alan and these girls attend middle school together. Alan's dad remembers getting shot down by several girls during high school and college, so he thinks it's great that Alan is getting all this attention. After each call, he asks Alan about the girl and often suggests that Alan ask her out.

Other parents allow their young teenagers to date because they naively believe that their teens are different from other kids their age, "more mature," and can be trusted. Some parents even allow a young daughter to date a boy who is three or four years older.

Last night I overheard a man describe a situation in which his fifteen-year-old daughter wanted permission for her boyfriend to come over to the house after school to study; neither the mom nor the dad would be home. This man and his wife told their daughter, "We've raised you to know what's right and wrong, and we want to trust you. If we can't trust you by now, then we've done a pretty bad job. This is a good time to see if you really can be trusted." Then they said yes.

The reasoning of this mom and dad sounds, well, so reasonable, doesn't it? And the situation may be perfectly innocent, with the two teens doing nothing but studying. (I know the girl and her boyfriend, and both seem to be good kids.) But these parents have forgotten the strength of the teenage sex drive and the power of lust. Even if these parents trust their daughter, do they know enough about the boy to trust him? They are placing their daughter and her boyfriend in a very tempting situation. It would be like placing a plate of warm chocolate chip cookies in front of six-year-olds and then giving them the same speech about trust. Regardless of the six-year-olds' good intentions, I doubt that it would be very long before the look and smell of those cookies would silence their restraint, and they would begin nibbling the tempting delights.

Unfortunately, I have seen many parents make similar mistakes with their kids. Either they are naive about pressure, temptation, immaturity, and human nature, or they are unaware of the actual actions, motives, and tendencies of *their* children. School administrators and police can give scores of examples of parents who are shocked when confronted with their "darling" teens' behavior. I will never forget the devastating look of betrayal and disappointment when a mom learned that her "good Christian" daughter was pregnant. Sometimes we parents can't see the forest for the trees; that is, we are so close to the situation and blinded by our love for our kids that we can't see what they are like or what they are doing. We ignore the clues or explain them away.

Parents need to take off the blinders and take a realistic look at their children and what is happening in their lives.

The Facts

Several facts help us see the dating issue in perspective, especially for young teenagers. It is important to understand that eventually children are going to act their age. In other words, regardless of how much older a sixth-grade girl looks, she is still a sixth grader and will act like one. No matter how mature a sixteen-year-old boy looks and acts, he still is sixteen; eventually he will act (and drive) like it. This is not to denigrate young teens; it's not wrong to be young and to act one's age. However, as adults and parents, we should not subject our children to undue responsibilities and pressures. I understand that there is a fine line here. On the one hand we need to give our children increased responsibilities as they age and prove themselves to be responsible, and we need to help them move toward maturity and independence. On the other hand these responsibilities must be commensurate with their abilities and needs. We do no one a favor by overrating him or her. That simply sets the stage for failure.

The fact is that young teens are not equipped mentally or emotionally to deal with one-on-one dating. By encouraging or permitting it, we set them up for failure and even disaster.

In addition to the developmental issues, we have the hard facts of research. Studies have shown that the earlier kids date, the more likely they are to become sexually active. This should be obvious. Experienced daters know the lines to use and how to respond. And let's face it, once teenagers have traveled down the physical road, they will be able to get to that point on the road more easily and more quickly with the next romantic interest. Remember when you held hands the first time on a date? It was thrilling, sweaty palms and all. Eventually, however, holding hands wasn't a big deal. But that first kiss, now that was something! Eventually, a simple kiss wasn't as exciting either. It only makes sense that the sooner young people start down that physical road, the sooner they will reach the end. And research about teen sexual behavior supports this view.

FREQUENT AND EARLY DATING

It has long been reported that frequent and early dating are connected with early sexual experience. This analysis [Values and Choices study] confirms it. Another of the factors connected with a student's statement that he or she expects to be sexually active as a teenager is the amount of dating a young person has done.

—*Source*[1]

So, What's a Parent to Do?

What are the choices we face as our teenagers move into the dating experience? We can give in to the pressure we feel from kids, school, society, and other parents. We can let our young teenagers date, thinking it's cute that they are entering the adult world. We can push them into dating because we didn't have successful dating experiences. We can forbid them to date until they are twenty-one years old. (Try that one.) Or we can establish some guidelines that will help our teenagers ease into the dating experience and derive full benefit from developing opposite-sex relationships.

41

The Choice

The choices here can be especially tough because they come into direct conflict with the world's values and pressures. Before diving into the choices, however, let's look at a few important truths.

The Truths

You are not alone in your confusion. In fact, all good parents wonder when they should allow their sons and daughters to date. Your struggle is normal.

You are not the last strict parent on the earth. You may be more strict in some areas, but other parents (in your church and in your neighborhood) are more strict than you are in other areas. When kids use the argument that a friend's parents are more understanding and lenient than you are, remember that children are very selective in choosing their evidence. Or perhaps they know only a little about another family's lifestyle and would cringe at some of their rules. You aren't weird.

It is more important to do what is right than what others think you should do. Adults like to admonish teenagers to resist peer pressure and to make responsible choices. Yet we adults often give in to pressures from society and our peers. As a good parent, you should do what is best for your children, even if it isn't popular. As a Christian, you should do what God wants, even if it goes against the cultural current.

Children will look for acceptance and love elsewhere if they don't find it at home. Studies have shown that kids from broken homes or homes with absent parents, especially absent fathers, are more likely to jump into serious and sexual relationships. Children need their parents to model a healthy female-male relationship. They also need massive doses of affection. Hug your teenagers often, and tell them that you love them.

REACH OUT AND TOUCH

Don't back off touching your children. Daughters need their fathers to continue to touch them appropriately, even after they have gone through puberty and have developed physically. Of course you should be careful not to embarrass your daughter in public, in front of her friends, but a hug is almost always appropriate. A problem develops when a father treats his daughter differently after she reaches adolescence. Many teenage girls feel rejected when their dads stop touching them after their bodies begin to change. . . .

Genuine acceptance from Dad is important, not only for the momentary feeling of security it provides, but also because it opens the pathway to healthy relationships in the future. A daughter's first attempts to reach across the sex barrier to please men will be with her own father. She needs to know from him if she is acceptable, if she is attractive, and if her conversation is intelligent. If her dad applauds her mental and spiritual attributes at an early age, she will have the confidence that she doesn't have to rely on shallow sex appeal to attract young men in her growing up years. If her father continues to affirm her in a proper way, she will become convinced that she has importance as a person, not as a sex object.

—Chuck Aycock and Dave Veerman
From Dad, with Love[2]

The Choices

You don't have to give in to the dating dilemma. I suggest that you make the following tough choices about your teenagers' dating relationships.

Choice 1: Set the Dating Age at Sixteen. The sixteenth birthday isn't the magical moment at which children suddenly attain the maturity needed to handle serious relationships. Turning sixteen also does not mean that if teenagers have made it this far, they won't ever have conflicts or problems with members of the opposite sex. Sixteen does seem, however, to be the right age for allowing kids to begin one-on-one dating. Consider these reasons:

- Most sixteen-year-olds have outgrown their early adolescent immaturity and have entered middle adolescence.
- Most sixteen-year-olds have had at least one year of high school, so they are familiar with the school building and activities, have met many new students, and have established new friendships.
- In many states, sixteen-year-olds are allowed to obtain a driver's license. This rite of passage signals a step into the adult world and the assuming of other privileges and responsibilities.
- Most sixteen-year-olds will have about two years to date during high school—usually enough time to learn how and whom to date.

EARLY DATING

I wish my parents had been more strict about dating. I went out with a guy for a few months when I was fifteen, and I realize that I was too young. I don't think I was ready for opening my heart that far, and I got hurt. I wish they had made me wait until I was sixteen.

—Emily, sixteen-year-old female

When our daughters were very young, I would joke with them and say something like, "Remember, boys are yucky!" (Perhaps I was serious, worrying even then about my little girls being hurt or not wanting them to grow up.) In serious moments, at the right time, Gail and I would explain that they could begin dating at sixteen. Having heard and understood our feelings years before they developed an interest in boys, the girls neither chafed under nor rebelled against the rule. At times they didn't like it and lobbied for an exception or two, but they understood that we were standing firm.

Don't wait for junior high school to bring up this subject. Explain this rule when the kids are young. Then, as they get older and become interested in members of the opposite sex, remind them of the rule and give your reasons.

I need to add quickly that this dating limit will be much easier for some parents to enforce than others because children differ so much. Some teens are naturally shy or are late bloomers. For these kids, waiting until age sixteen to date is no sweat because they may lack the courage to ask, may not get asked, or may be rejected if they were to ask. The toughest situations involve girls and guys who have physically matured earlier than most of their peers and who run with the popular group on campus. The pressure will be greatest on them and, thus, on their parents.

- Although only a freshman, Gregg plays varsity football. He attracts girls without even trying. They write him notes, call him, and even ask him out.
- Gayle is still in eighth grade, but her sparkling personality, cute smile, and shapely body have caught the eye (and imagination) of several high school juniors and seniors at the high school basketball games and at church.
- As a sophomore cheerleader, Francine regularly performs her routine in front of the entire student body. Cheerleaders are expected to go to the after-game dances and especially homecoming. Almost all of the other girls on her squad have steady boyfriends.

- Mario has an unusually mature singing voice for a fifteen-year-old, so he has been the featured soloist for the choir and was one of the male leads in the musical. Lately he has received a lot of attention from the female cast members.

From the young person's perspective, the negative points about waiting until sixteen to date swirl around peers and popularity. But on the positive side, having that rule takes the pressure off them, especially when they are being hounded by undesirables. "I can't. My parents won't let me date until I'm sixteen" can be an escape, an easy way out of a sticky social situation.

Set the dating age at sixteen and hold to it, even when that special person shows interest in your son or daughter and homecoming is on the horizon.

Choice 2: Help Your Teenagers Ease into Dating. Actually, this process should begin well before your teenagers reach age sixteen as you encourage them to get involved in wholesome activities that include boys and girls together. I must emphasize the word *wholesome.* Make sure the activity helps your teenagers and that the opposite-sex friendships are serendipitous; that is, they are *by-products* of the events and not the focus. Church and community youth groups, choirs, and athletic teams can be excellent places to learn and have fun with members of the other sex. When I led the junior high group at church, usually the boys would sit together on one side of the room and the girls on the other. Often for our games, I would capitalize on that division and feature boys-versus-girls competition. At other times, however, I would mix the sexes for teams or discussion groups. Although most of the kids held no romantic thoughts, at least they had the opportunity to get to know members of the opposite sex.

Waiting until sixteen doesn't mean that boys and girls should have no contact beforehand. You *don't* want to give your teenager the message that boys (or girls) really are "yucky." Ideally your daughter or son eventually will date and marry a wonderful person. So look for wholesome group activities.

Also if you haven't already helped your children discover the biblical principles about opposite-sex relationships when they were younger, it's not too late to begin now.

- For guidelines about *sex,* see Exodus 20:14; Deuteronomy 23:17-18; Proverbs 5:18-20; 1 Corinthians 6:18–7:11; 1 Thessalonians 4:1-8.
- For teachings about *love,* see John 3:16; 13:1-17, 34-35; 1 Corinthians 13:1-13; 1 John 4:7-12.
- For guidelines about *relationships with non-Christians,* see Psalm 1:1; 26:4-5; 2 Corinthians 6:14-18.
- For teachings about *temptation,* see 1 Corinthians 10:12-13; Hebrews 4:14-16; James 1:2-4, 13-15; 2 Peter 2:9.
- For guidelines about *marriage,* see Genesis 2:18-25; Matthew 5:31-32; 19:7-12; Mark 10:2-12; 1 Corinthians 7:1-40; Ephesians 5:21-33; Hebrews 13:4.

(Note: the *Life Application Bible for Students* [Tyndale House Publishers] is a tremendous resource for help on these topics. Check out the "Life-Changer Index" in the back.)

The Bible makes it quite clear that Christians should not become entangled in long-term, contractual relationships with non-Christians. Certainly this includes marriage, the closest human relationship. The differences between the Christian's and the non-Christian's focus, perspective, values, morals, and ultimate allegiance are too great to overlook or overcome. Many Christian young people believe that they can date those who don't share their commitment to Christ because "It's just a date. We're not serious or anything!" Yet no one can predict how a relationship will develop, especially when emotions and sexual attraction are involved. Marrying a non-Christian always begins with dating one.

When Christian teenagers commit to dating only people who share their faith and values, they feel added pressure, especially in public schools. Christian students can feel as if there are few, if any, possibilities. Every situation and family is unique, and you may feel the pressure, empathize with your teenagers, and allow them to date non-Christians from time to time. But I encourage you to make it the exception. Pray with your teenagers about this area of life; ask God to bring the right people into their lives. Discussing and praying about this issue early with your children will prepare them for the dating years. It will help your teenagers set and keep their standards high.

When each of our daughters turned sixteen, they insisted on getting the coveted driver's license *on that day.* That's all right for driving a car, but it shouldn't be the same with dating. In other words, hitting that momentous mark on the calendar shouldn't signal that teenagers suddenly have complete freedom to date whomever and whenever they want. Remember, in order to get a driver's license, teenagers have to take a driver's education course. Then they practice for a few weeks or months on a *permit,* under the watchful eye of an experienced driver. Wouldn't it be great if the same were true for dating? First, the young person would have to take a course for a semester; then, after passing a written test, he or she would be issued a permit.

We know that won't happen. But what can we as parents do to help our teenagers ease into dating? Emphasize group dates.

Encourage your teenagers to participate in fun activities with a group of friends, not just doing things only as a couple. Explain this "easing in" process to your teenager, and then brainstorm together about creative dating options. And together look for groups and activities where they can meet Christian teenagers. Some examples on your list might include church youth group, church conferences and conventions, Campus Life, Young Life, Fellowship of Christian Athletes, or summer camp.

CHOOSING A DATE

I teach kids that Galatians 5:19-23 gives relevant advice for choosing the right person to date. Verses 19-21 describe those who are controlled by their own selfish desires. These people are immoral (verse 19); that is, they go too far physically. Bad company corrupts good morals, all the time! According to spiritual gravity, it is easier to pull someone down than to pull someone up. The first thing to check is whether this person goes too far physically.

The second characteristic in verse 19 deals with impurity—thinking about sex in an ungodly manner. The human mind is the most important sex organ. If you sow a thought, you will reap an attitude; sow an attitude, reap a habit; sow a habit, reap a lifestyle; sow a lifestyle, reap a destiny. It all starts in the mind.

The third characteristic is sensuality or talking about sex in an ungodly manner. You can't read a person's mind, but you can listen to him or her talk. If a person is always dwelling on sex, he or she will talk about it. Remember, out of the mouth come the issues of the heart. Look at the other examples of a "fleshly" person that continue through verse 21—check them out. Don't date that kind of person.

In contrast, look at the qualities listed in verses 22-23. This is the kind of person to date: loving (true to commitments), joyful (happy on the inside), peaceful (assured of God's control), patient (willing to wait), kind (considerate of others), good (desirous to do what is right), faithful (dependable), gentle (sensitive to another's needs), self-controlled (submitting personal desires to God's desires).

—Bill Jones
author, speaker, and president of Crossover Communications

Also, as we discussed in the previous chapter, encourage your teenagers to bring their same-sex and opposite-sex friends to your house. Put on a party, provide videos and snacks, let them listen to their favorite music. Make your home a social center.

Choice 3: Monitor the Dates. When you do allow your teens to date as just a couple, learn as much as you can about the date beforehand, especially if you have a daughter and the boy will be driving. And let your daughter know that you expect to meet and talk with her date when he comes to pick her up. I have vivid memories of meeting my dates' parents, especially their fathers. I was nervous, but meeting them helped me remember that each girl was someone's daughter, that she was part of a family, and that I could not treat her lightly. Today, Gail and I want to meet our daughters' dates, not because we want to interrogate the young men, but because we want to get to know them, to let them get to know us, and to help them realize that we care about our daughters.

HEALTHY RELATIONSHIPS

Helping your daughter or son develop healthy male-female relationships is *vital* to her or his development. A key is to ask your adolescent to think about *group dates*—four to eight people going out. A second key is to approach a dating relationship as first a friendship.

—Kara Eckmann
Director of College Ministry, Lake Avenue Church, Pasadena

For a big event, such as homecoming or prom, you may want to get together with the date's parents and discuss your expectations for the evening (cost, curfew, rules, etc.). Communication will clear the air of potential misunderstandings, and presenting a united front will help your teenagers know what is expected of them.

For *every* date, insist that you know what the couple is planning to do. For example, "We are going to the basketball game and then out for pizza" or "We are going to the movie and then to the Carlsons' house." Don't be afraid to ask questions. For example, "What movie are you planning to see?" or "Will Mr. and Mrs. Carlson be home?" Make sure the answers match your values. In other words, if you don't allow your kids to attend R-rated movies, then don't make an exception just because it's a date. Also, set a realistic curfew, and insist that your teens check in with you if plans change (for example, the car breaks down) or if they choose to change the plans.

Besides monitoring individual dates, be sure to monitor long-term relationships. Watch for signs of sexual involvement or unhealthy relationships. Don't be paranoid and assume the worst of your teenagers; on the other hand, don't be naive and overlook the obvious. Does your teen show a consuming interest in the other person? Has your son or daughter cut off other friends because of increased involvement with a girlfriend or boyfriend? Has your teen become secretive and stopped talking to you about his or her relationship? These are warning signs, signaling the time for intervention. The signs could warn of sexual involvement, self-destructive behavior (smoking, drinking, or drugs), a possessive or abusive relationship, or some other problem.

Recently, a friend told me of discovering that her daughter, Teri, had been in an abusive dating relationship in high school. This mother had seen nothing unusual; in fact, the young man had always been very polite around her and her husband. After a dramatic incident, my friend began to question her daughter about the boy and their relationship.

> One evening Michael burst through our front door, calling loudly for my husband and me. When we came downstairs, he blurted, "I can't find Teri! I can't find Teri!" Then he collapsed in a fetal position on the floor and began to sob uncontrollably. We calmed him down and got him to tell us exactly what had happened.
>
> Michael explained that a couple of miles from our house, during an argument with Teri, he lost his temper, stopped the car, and told Teri to get out. Then he drove off. A few blocks later, he calmed down. But when he drove back to get her, she wasn't there. He drove up and down the street but couldn't find her anywhere. So he panicked and drove to our house. (Later, we learned that although Teri was quite shook up after Michael had driven off, she knew where she was and had started for home through the back streets.)
>
> My husband went with Michael, and together they found Teri walking home. In questioning Michael afterward, we learned that he had come from an abusive home and frequently had angry outbursts himself. As he left, we encouraged him to get counseling.
>
> Later, Teri told us how possessive Michael had become and how he would harm her physically from time to time. For example, he would grab both her arms and squeeze tightly, and twice he actually hit her. Often he would get angry and yell. At other times, he would lecture her.
>
> That was the end of that relationship. Looking back,

I can see several signs that should have tipped me off. First, when Michael and Teri would talk, Teri would always assume a very submissive position. For example, she would sit on the ground when he sat on the hood of his car, or she would sit on the floor at his feet when he sat in the chair. At other times, Teri would step back, almost behind him when they were with us.

Second, he never showed any affection toward Teri although they had been dating regularly for several weeks. There was no holding hands, arm around the shoulders, or good-bye hug. At times, I wondered if he even liked her.

Third, he was excessively polite to my husband and me. He said all the right words and was always so patronizing. He reminded us of Eddie Haskell on *Leave It to Beaver.*

Finally, I did hear him raise his voice in anger from time to time when he was talking to Teri, but then he would calm down. I should have seen the signs and said something to Teri, but I ignored them, assuming that everything was fine.

Fortunately, these parents became aware of the situation before it had worsened.

Monitor your teenagers' dates and relationships. Don't be nosy, but don't be foolish and ignore the obvious. Also, don't assume that because the date is a Christian that everything is fine; Christian teenagers have hormones, emotions, and weaknesses too.

Choice 4: Use Dating as a Teaching Opportunity. Dating provides an excellent opportunity to teach responsibility and trust.

As you ask your questions about the potential date and remind your teenagers of your dating guidelines and rules, explain that you are motivated by love and concern. It's not that you don't *trust* your teenagers; you don't trust others very much. For example, we live in a Chicago suburb. Gail and I would not allow our sixteen-year-old daughter, Dana, to go into the city on a date, not because we don't trust her, but because we know the city. It can be a dangerous place for young, inexperienced high school students who have been driving for only a few months and who don't know their way around.

Also explain that trust is easily lost and then difficult to win back. For example, someone might trust a friend with a valuable

AVOID DATING HEADACHES

Big dating events—like homecoming or prom—often result in big headaches for parents and even bigger heartaches for teens. To minimize the suffering for all involved, adopt the P.R.O.M. strategy:

Pray. We need not worry (Philippians 4:6-7). We have a good and caring heavenly Father (1 Peter 5:7) who invites us to bring our concerns to him (Luke 18:1-8).

Remember. The next time your daughter is obsessed about getting a dress (or a date!) or your son wants to spend $300 (or more!) to impress his prom date, think back to your own adolescence. Try to recall those strong feelings and make the effort to be understanding.

Offer. Tell your dating son or daughter that you (and some other parents) are willing to "cater" their big fancy meal. Pull out the candles, fine china, and all the stops. Make it a fun night they'll never forget.

Maximize. The "dating years" provide us with a myriad of natural opportunities to teach our children about what matters most in life (Deuteronomy 6). We need to make the most of these "teachable moments."

—Len Woods
Minister to Students, Christ Community Church, Ruston, Louisiana

possession. If that friend loses or damages that possession, the person will find it difficult to trust the friend with anything else right away. In the same way, you trust your teenagers; that is, you expect them to tell you the truth and to adhere to your guidelines and obey your rules. As your teenagers gain maturity and experience and as they prove that they can handle freedom and responsibility, you will trust them with *more* freedom and responsibility. This will mean widening the scope of possible dating activities and moving the curfew to a later hour. If, however, you learn that the trust has been broken, you will limit their freedom.

Initial dating experiences also provide tremendous opportunities for teaching about male-female relationships, respect, and sex. I would hope that you have taught your children about sex well before the teenage years, but there's nothing like hormones, locker-room talk, and dating pressure to move sex from a topic of discussion to a felt need. Let your teenagers know how to treat the other person with respect. Encourage your teenagers to stay away from tempting and pressure-packed situations (such as parking, being in a house with no parents home, watching a suggestive video, double-dating with a sexually active couple, etc.). Explain sexual harassment and how to respond to it.

Discussing sex with your teenagers won't be easy, so think through your plan. Don't simply blurt out a question after school, after a date, or at dinner. A better strategy would be to take your teenagers out for breakfast or lunch on a Saturday. During the course of conversation, ask them about how things are going in their dating relationships. If your teenagers don't offer any information, describe some common sexual pressures faced by kids, perhaps even some of your frustrating dating experiences. Let your teenagers know that you want them to be open and honest with you and that you want to help. Then reaffirm your trust.

Encourage the youth ministers at your church to hit this topic head-on. Christian ministries and publishers have produced a number of curricula that include videos and books about sex and dating. The *True Love Waits* campaign, in which young people pledge sexual abstinence until marriage, has been outstanding, promoting chastity and giving kids permission to do what is right and responsible.[3]

If you learn of a problem (a friend saw your car parked at the forest preserve late last Friday night; your teenagers are becoming secretive; you heard them sneak in well after curfew; or you found telltale stains on the clothes), intervene immediately, with love. Explain what you heard or what you have seen, then allow your teenagers to give their side of the story. If you are convinced of disobedience or inappropriate sexual activity, hold the line. Exercise your strong will. Don't yell, scream, and blast the teenagers. But don't let them get away with it, either. Disobedience is too important to overlook or minimize. Problems and mistakes also give you the chance to teach about God's love and forgiveness.

Choice 5: Talk with Other Parents. Remember that you are not alone in this struggle. Many other parents also wonder how to deal with teenage dating and sex. Get together with Christian parents and discuss the situation together. You may even want to form a support group consisting of parents of teenagers. You can share resources, ideas, and answers, and you can pray for each other.

* * *

In our sex-obsessed culture, we can become intimidated and psyched out when even thinking about our children dating. Instead of foolishly assuming that our kids are more emotionally and spiritually mature and can handle the boy-girl thing or instead of giving in to the prevailing pressure, we should hold the line on dating. The choices will be tough, but they are vital: set the dating age at sixteen; help teenagers ease into dating; monitor the dates; use dating as an opportunity to teach; and talk with other parents.

THINK IT THROUGH

1. What examples of pressuring kids to date do you see on television, at school, or from your teenagers' peers?
2. What lessons from your early dating experiences can you pass on to your teens?
3. What can you and your spouse do to prepare your younger children for positive relationships with the opposite sex?
4. What are (or will be) your dating rules?
5. What do you hope dating will accomplish for your teenagers?
6. What can you do to help your teens know whom to date?
7. What resources will help your kids resist premarital sex?
8. How can you help your teenagers show respect to their dating partners?
9. In what ways does your relationship with your spouse model respect for the opposite sex and a healthy, God-honoring outlook on sex?
10. What reasons will you give for insisting on sixteen as the age to begin dating?

CHAPTER **3**

"Church? . . . Boring!"

> *"Frankly, I think this calls for*
> *some good, old-fashioned*
> *parental interference."*
> —Ozzie to Harriet
> from "Rick's Raise"

"ELLEN, ARE YOU READY?"

Silence. Quickly walking from the kitchen to the foot of the stairs, Sandy Johnson calls again, this time a bit louder. "Ellen?"

No answer. Walking up a few stairs to the landing, she sees the closed door to her daughter's room and hears the familiar sounds of stereo music. A few stairs later, standing outside Ellen's room, she raises her voice even louder: "Ellen, get out here!"

Seconds later, the door opens, revealing a defiant thirteen-year-old. "What?" Ellen mutters with a scowl, looking out at her mother.

"I've been calling you for five minutes. You know it's time to go to youth group. Are you ready?" Sandy Johnson says with an edge in her voice as she walks into her daughter's room.

Ellen folds her arms, glares, and announces, "I don't want to go. Youth group is stupid!"

Picking up the pace and returning the glare, Ellen's mother responds, "What do you mean you don't want to go? And how can you say youth group is stupid? You've always enjoyed church and all the youth activities! I don't know what's gotten into you lately."

After a long sigh, Ellen answers, "Oh, come on, Mom. Church is so booooring!"

The argument escalates to shouts and accusations. Furious and frustrated, Sandy Johnson finally yells something like, "If you're not going to youth group, then you're not talking on the phone or listening to music either, so you may as well go to bed, and your father and I are going to talk about this, and you had better change your attitude, young lady!" Then she slams the door behind her and stomps downstairs.

This isn't the Johnsons' first argument over church, and it won't be the last. For the past few months, every Sunday has meant a conflict over some aspect of the family's spiritual life. First it was after-dinner devotions. Ellen slumped in her chair and rolled her eyes when her dad pulled out the Bible. Next on the list was the family dinner at church. Ellen announced that it was just for old people and little kids. Then Sunday school became the target. Ellen's teacher, Mr. Short, had said she was disruptive and disrespectful in class. Lately the struggle has been over the worship time. Ellen wants to sit with her friends, but her parents want the family to sit together.

PARTICIPATION IN CHURCH LIFE

According to Effective Christian Education data, in the mainline churches, participation in church life begins to decrease as early as seventh, eighth, and ninth grades. For many, it never recovers.

—Source[1]

Negative body language, deep sighs, descriptions of church as "boring, stupid, and dumb," and a defiant attitude have made each church event a battleground. Ted and Sandy Johnson haven't a clue about what to do. Until six months ago, Ellen, along with her younger brother and sister, would grab her Bible and hop willingly, almost joyfully, into the minivan on Sunday mornings. And she was thrilled about being able to join the junior high youth group when she started sixth grade. But what a difference a year makes! Her attitude has turned 180 degrees.

Although the parental struggles are real—and painful—Ellen's experiences and expressions are fairly typical for seventh graders. Ted and Sandy have *not* made some terrible parenting mistake; they are *not* raising a monster.

The Challenge

Teenagers experience tremendous changes in every area of life, but the physical, social, and mental changes in junior high school students are almost cataclysmic. Many of these changes influence kids' attitudes toward life, including their attitude toward church and related activities.

As children approach adolescence, they grow physically, with some gaining several pounds and inches in a few months. Perhaps the most extreme physical change, however, occurs inside their bodies as hormones begin to kick in. Often early adolescents don't understand this physical transformation and can be frustrated and confused by their bodies. Girls tend to grow faster than boys. Many eighth-grade girls feel like giants as they tower over their male peers, while the guys feel like shrimps. These years also feature pimples, braces, and awkwardness. No wonder junior high students fidget and squirm in church. They are uncomfortable and can't control their bodies.

A second major change occurs in the social area. In addition to heightened awareness of the opposite sex, adolescents experiment with a variety of roles and relationships. Friends mean everything. Like wolves, adolescents tend to travel in packs. They also can become protective of their territory as they hurl cruel and hateful comments at perceived rivals. Social intrigues fill their conversation: who's "going out" with whom, what so-and-so said, how he or she is such a jerk, and so forth.

Changes are occurring in the mental area as well. When children are young, they think concretely. They tend to accept statements literally, to take them at face value. And they appreciate descriptions in black and white, no in-between shades of gray. As teenagers grow older, they make the transition into the adult world, where people think conceptually, use analogies to describe realities, appreciate symbols and subtleties, and have learned to think matters through in order to come to a suitable compromise.

These changes conspire to make church a difficult proposition, especially for younger adolescents. Consider these additional factors:

- Many churches provide junior church and children's bulletins for younger children, who aren't expected to find adult worship very interesting. Early adolescents, however, are told to sit quietly, pay attention, and participate fully in the service. Yet their changing bodies make sitting still a real challenge, and most of the content of the service deals in profound *concepts,* especially when the pastor refers to the original Greek or Hebrew, famous theologians, doctrine, and denominational distinctives. Church really *can* be boring for early adolescents.

- Most churches draw from a number of communities and neighborhoods. So the youth groups will include young people from many schools. Thus, Sunday school and youth group are not natural groupings of students. Even a small church may have kids from four or five different middle schools and junior high schools. Considering early adolescents' social changes, they won't necessarily be drawn to the group because most of their friends from school or the neighborhood won't be there.

- Many publishers of Sunday school curricula don't fully consider early adolescents' developmental issues when designing their programs. Most early adolescents still think *concretely.* When faced with lessons focused on Christian *concepts,* teens are unable to connect. Their developmental needs are ignored, and they are expected to listen to a lecture or to dig out the timeless truths from the Bible on their own.

- Junior high Sunday school classes and youth groups usually have boys and girls together and kids in sixth through eighth grade. Such a wide range of physical sizes, emotional and spiritual needs, and levels of maturity leads to some unusual social dynamics. Like Ellen, many junior high students can be described as "disruptive and disrespectful."

With all of the changes in adolescence, it is easy to see why kids like Ellen say that church is boring and that they don't want to participate in church activities. Sadly, Ellen is not alone. I have seen many teenagers attend confirmation classes during the junior high years, then stop going to church "after confirmation." It is ironic that after being "confirmed in the faith," they "leave the faith." It's as if by being confirmed, they pleased their parents and then were free to do as they wished.

The Conflict

Most Christian parents want their children to be involved in church, so they bring their babies, toddlers, and little ones to the nursery, Sunday school, Vacation Bible School, kids' clubs,

BASIC TEENAGE RELIGIOUS BELIEFS AND PRACTICES
Percentage of all teens who
Believe in God or universal spirit 95%
Believe God loves them 93%
Believe Jesus Christ is God or Son of God 86%
Personally experienced presence of God 29%
Believe there is a heaven 91%
Believe there is a hell 76%
Believe in life after death 67%
Pray alone frequently 42%
Go to Sunday school 41%
Belong to church-sponsored youth group 36%
Read Bible at least weekly 36%
Listened to religious program on radio or TV last month 35%
Have confidence in organized religion 52%
Believe religion is increasing its influence on American life . . 40%
Consider own religious beliefs very important 39%
Consider religion more important than parents do 27%
Believe religion can answer today's problems 25%

*—America's Youth in the
1990s*[2]

and other activities. Barring a total breakdown or disaster, most young children probably will enjoy church, making their parents happy.

When these same kids grow up and suddenly sour on the Sunday experience, parents are puzzled, frustrated, and confused. They aren't sure how to respond.

Many parents react with anger, with each confrontation dissolving quickly into a shouting match. And because middle school students often speak in extremes, they can say hurtful things like, "I hate this family!" or "You treat me like dirt!" or "I can never please you!" Parents may react to the shouting with even more shouting, escalating the conflict until they announce that they have grounded the son or daughter "for life" or a similar punishment.

At other times, teenagers may try reasoning with the parent, explaining that a friend doesn't "have to" go to church, implying that their parents are extremely strict—more strict, in fact, than any of their friends' parents. (Note: This line of reasoning appears in many other parent-child disagreements.) Unsettled by this information and intimidated by their young teens' outbursts, many parents give in to the teenagers' demands and allow them to sleep in on Sundays after a late Saturday activity, miss Sunday school, skip youth group, and doodle through the worship service.

GETTING IN THE SWIM

When I was a teenager, I argued with my mom virtually every day about going to swim practice. I also argued with her about going to church. In both cases, once I arrived, I enjoyed myself. In fact, I recently learned that one day I so vehemently opposed my mom about attending swim practice that she secretly observed one of my practices from outside the pool gate to see why I detested it. She says that the entire time I was laughing, splashing water at my friends, and looking as if I was having a thoroughly good time.

From this experience, I recommend two steps. First, try to observe your teenagers' youth meetings. Chances are, your kids are not as bored as they would like you to think they are. Plus, seeing the meetings may assuage some of your guilt about forcing them to go.

Second, do whatever you can to help your teenagers build strong and positive friendships at church. Drive them to friends' houses. Invite their friends over. Provide money for movies, dinners, amusement parks—whatever it takes to strengthen your adolescents' social ties in the youth ministry. I'm more and more convinced that ministering to adolescents socially will enable and enhance ministry to them spiritually.
                                                        —Kara Eckmann
                                                Director of College Ministry,
                                              Lake Avenue Church, Pasadena

Some parents just get tired of all the bickering and fighting and may say something like, "You at least have to finish confirmation. Then you can decide for yourself."

Other parents, wanting desperately to respond in the right way, try to be open-minded about church. Realizing that in four to seven years their teenagers will be out of the home and on their own, they allow their teenagers to choose where and when they will attend church services and activities. Parents may say something like, "We think it's important for Jon to make his own decisions and to choose his own church. We don't want to *force* him." These parents may even encourage their teenagers to church shop, to search for a compatible youth group or one where many of their school friends attend.

Several problems emerge from this line of thinking and responding:

1. Teenagers, especially early adolescents, don't understand themselves, how they are feeling, or what they are saying. As I noted before, teenagers tend to speak in extremes. Eavesdrop on a conversation between adolescents. It will be sprinkled liberally with words like *stupid, dumb, love,* and *hate.* Teens' emotions also fluctuate greatly. They can be happy and sad in almost the same sentence. They can insist on something and then contradict themselves a minute later. Thus, it is usually a mistake to take what early adolescents say literally and to respond accordingly.

2. Teenagers, especially early adolescents, challenge parents, teachers, coaches, and others in authority and push against the limits. It's almost as if they are saying, "I'm a teenager. It's my job to give you a hard time." But no matter how much they push and argue, *teenagers, especially early adolescents, need limits.* And deep down they know it. Teenagers respect school administrators, coaches, teachers, and parents who keep control of their school, team, class, or family, enforce the rules, and exercise discipline. Adults do not do kids any favors by allowing them to do as they please.

3. Teenagers, especially early adolescents, don't have the information, experience, and maturity to make major decisions on their own. For example, what kind of food would typical teenagers choose to eat? When would they go to bed every night? How would they do in school? These are transition years during which kids need to be taught personal discipline and life skills. As they mature and reach the last couple of years in high school, they should be self-disciplined and able to make responsible decisions.

4. Teenagers, especially early adolescents, want a close family, and they appreciate their parents' involvement in their lives. Assuming that teenagers don't want them around, many parents withdraw from their adolescents. And let's face it, teens can be obnoxious and not fun to be with; it takes a lot of emotional energy to hang in there with them. Dads, especially, seem to disengage from early adolescents, suddenly becoming busy at the office or at church. But during these years, our kids need us more than ever. And remember, we still have the responsibility as parents to care for and nurture our children.

So, What's a Parent to Do?

What are the tough choices we must make with our teenagers? How can we keep them growing spiritually and involved with church when they find it boring? Do we force them to go and pay no attention to their perceptions? Do we nag them? Do we let them choose whether or not they will attend church?

Be prepared to be strong willed in this area. No other area in your teenagers' lives has such long-term significance as does maintaining a healthy spiritual life.

TOO BUSY TO PRACTICE

I have often wondered what would happen if football coaches approached their work as most youth ministers are expected to do. For example, I wonder what would happen if, when a player was too busy to show up for practice, the understanding coach simply said, "We'll miss you. I hope you'll be able to make it next week sometime."

Imagine the players leaving practice and hearing the smiling coach say, "Thanks for coming. I hope you'll come back tomorrow."

If a football team operated like a typical youth ministry, we might expect concerned parents to call the coach, saying, "Can you tell me what's been going on in practice? My son says it's boring, and he doesn't want to come anymore. I was wondering, could you make it a little more fun for them? And by the way, you may want to talk to the coach at the school across town. He seems to have the right idea." The coach may send out quarterly questionnaires about what the players would like to change about the team. (I can just imagine the answers: "shorter practices," "more winning.")

A coach, responding like a typical youth minister, may first feel guilty that the practices were not meeting the boy's needs, and he would try to adjust his program to suit this boy (and every other boy who complained). Between trying to keep everybody happy and giving every student a good experience, the coach would squeeze in a little football practice. And what kind of season would this coach have? It's a safe bet that the coach wouldn't be the only one who felt like a loser.

But this is the very way that most churches expect to run their youth ministries.
 —Mark DeVries
Family-Based Youth Ministry[3]

The Choice

I suggest that we be prepared to make tough choices in two areas: choices with our teenagers and choices in our own lives.

With Our Kids

The first set of choices involves our teenagers. First, I believe that the bottom line is this: Parents should insist that their teenagers maintain involvement with positive spiritual influences. This is not the time to relax the rules for Sunday or allow them to attend the church of their choice.

How we insist, however, is very important. I have had the opportunity to observe a wide variety of adults who work with teenagers: coaches, teachers, choir directors, youth leaders, and others. All of the good, effective ones have this in common: First, they clearly explain their rules; then, when the occasion requires it, they firmly and quietly enforce those rules. Remember, teen-

NONNEGOTIABLE

I tell parents that church attendance is not one of the negotiable issues in our family. Kids have no option when it comes to attending. This must be established early in the game, before the child hits the teen years.

I find two sources for teenagers' complaints about church. First is the young person who is not particularly interested in spiritual things; this kid sees church as cutting into other activities that he or she would rather do or as shining the "light" in his or her darkness. The second is the young person who would be involved or interested if the conditions were right.

Unfortunately, in a number of cases the kids are right: the church is boring, dumb, and irrelevant. That's when parents take action in several areas:

1. Put pressure on the church to become dynamic to kids: improve the youth ministry, start a contemporary worship service, allow kids to put together a rock worship team, attempt to communicate to the teenagers' world in the sermons.

2. Give young people opportunities to express their complaints and suggestions to the church. For example, take an evaluation from teenagers' points of view and make sure that the pastor sees it and responds to it.

3. Go to a church that has a vital interest in youth. This is drastic but sometimes necessary.
—Rick Bundschuh
author and copastor at
Kauai Christian Fellowship, Kauai, Hawaii

agers need and want limits to their behavior. What they don't want or need, however, are empty threats and verbal abuse.

During a youth meeting one of my volunteer helpers got so frustrated with an obnoxious seventh-grade boy that he called him a jerk. That may seem like a mild epithet, but the boy never came back to our meetings; our daughter told me that the boy had expressed how much he disliked that leader. When my helper lost his cool, he lost the boy. I can also remember times when I overreacted with one of our daughters by yelling at her during a disagreement. I got my way, of course, because I insisted on it as her father, but not without cost. Later I had to do some serious healing in the relationship.

Remember, "A gentle answer turns away wrath, but a harsh word stirs up anger" (Proverbs 15:1). And the apostle Paul reminds us, "Do not exasperate your children; instead, bring them up in the training and instruction of the Lord" (Ephesians 6:4).

Once we have insisted that our teenagers maintain spiritual involvement, how do we guide them to places where they will experience meaningful spiritual growth? We have several options. Obviously, the first one is church programs.

Church Programs. It is vitally important that our children are exposed to a variety of positive, Christian role models, teachers, and friends. As parents, we should be the primary influence in our children's lives, but *we need help.* Remember that in many ways you are engaged in a battle for your kids—so don't try to fight it alone. The church, your local body of believers, has programs, counsel, encouragement, information, and other resources for helping you be a better parent and for helping your teenagers mature in their faith. Take advantage of these resources. Of course, as we have noted earlier, this should begin well before the tumultuous teenage years.

If your teens are resistant to your church's programs, don't react immediately. My wife, Gail, and I lead the junior high ministry team at our church. At the beginning of the year, we meet with the parents of the potential members of our Sunday school class and youth group. In this meeting we warn them that their teenagers may use negative adjectives to describe church or may resist coming to our activities. After explaining the typical reasons for these reactions, we encourage parents not to take their kids literally and to bring them to our activities, even over their protests, and trust us to minister effectively with them. We tell these parents to see us if they have questions or problems with the youth group. We explain that they should not assume their teens' negative description or complaints are true. Almost without exception, the most vocal junior high objectors will settle into the group and have a great time, *once they get there*.

Of course, your adolescents' complaints may be legitimate. Not every youth group and Sunday school class will be an affirming place and a positive experience. The best way to deal with this, however, is to talk with the leaders, not to pull your teenagers out of the group. Work at keeping your teens involved in youth ministries.

Camps. While your church may be the primary place for your teenagers to receive spiritual nurture, it is not the only resource you have. You can find many other great organizations and programs for your teens. Some of the most valuable of these are summer camps, which kids usually begin attending at a fairly young age. I went to my first week of church camp, by myself, when I was eight years old. I wore the same clothes all week (my mom was shocked to discover that I hadn't disturbed any of the clothes in my suitcase), and I had a great time. For nine years I went to that camp, and I loved it! And that was in the "Dark

SERIOUS COMPLAINTS

If your teenager complains that the church you attend is boring, stupid, or dumb, don't dismiss this information completely. Your teen actually may be telling you something important about your church. Does the church you attend have a commitment to effective youth ministry? If not, you may need to consider whether or not your church is the right church for you and your family. I don't believe in "church hopping," but if I had to make a choice between a church that meets my needs and a church that meets the needs of my teenagers, I'd switch in a minute. The stakes are too high.

On the other hand, there may be nothing wrong at all with your church. Your teen may just be uninterested in spiritual things right now. This condition is normal and usually temporary. As a parent, I would be understanding but firm. "As a family, we will attend church every Sunday, whether or not we like it." If your teen isn't happy, that's OK. You should allow kids their feelings without criticism or punishment. But you don't have to allow behaviors that are unacceptable. And staying home from church is not acceptable.

—Wayne Rice
speaker, author, and cofounder
of Youth Specialties

Ages." Today, with great facilities and professional staff, camps offer parents and teenagers dozens of options. Besides traditional camps owned and operated by denominations, churches, Christian organizations, and Christian schools, independent camps have proliferated. Also many churches and organizations rent camping facilities and sponsor their own weeks of camp. And parents can choose from a variety of sports camps, music camps, and so forth, offering training and coaching from outstanding Christian teachers and coaches.

Teenagers will grow not only from the input from counselors and other staff but also through the chance to get away from their normal routine and environment. In the country, in the woods, in the mountains, by a lake, or by an ocean—removed from the noise and bustle of everyday life—teenagers can broaden their perspectives and take a fresh look at themselves and their relationship with God.

In the summer just before she began middle school, Kara, our older daughter, traveled alone to northern Wisconsin (five hours from home) for two weeks of camp. I was impressed with her courage and excited about what she would experience and learn. She attended that camp throughout her middle school years, each time taking along a friend or two. The next summer, however, she announced that she didn't want to go to camp. Gail and I weren't sure what was going on, but we were convinced of the importance of camp in Kara's life, so we signed her up for one week at a Christian camp a little closer to home. Up to the day we drove Kara to the camp, she expressed her disapproval. She didn't want to go to the "stupid camp." I remember leaving Kara at her cabin, giving her a good-bye hug, walking back to the car, and driving away. All the way home, Gail and I wondered whether we had done the right thing. A week later when we drove back to pick her up, she couldn't stop talking about the fun and activities. She introduced us to so many new friends she had made. She had loved it. The next summer we planned for her to attend a different camp. Much to our surprise, Kara was again resistant. However, once she got to the camp, she had a terrific time. She returned to that camp every summer of her high school years. Gail and I struggled with this choice. Fortunately, it worked out well. We are convinced of the value of summer camp. We've seen the effects in our kids' lives.

Besides residential camps, other camps offer older kids the chance to go rafting, climbing, rappelling, canoeing, hiking, spelunking, backpacking, and so forth. These high adventure trips stretch faith and build confidence. Teens also can go on a wide variety of short-term mission trips, on which they will serve others in a variety of ways: building churches in poor areas, tutoring underprivileged children, providing relief for victims of natural disasters, feeding the hungry, and sharing the gospel. Besides providing real help to very needy people, these trips broaden students' perspectives and heighten their sensitivity to poverty and hunger by exposing them to other cultures and to people in desperate need. These camps and trips are sponsored by individual churches and denominations as well as by independent organizations. Many are offered year-round, not just during the summer.

For good suggestions for summer camp experiences, ask your youth pastor and denominational leaders, or contact Young Life, Fellowship of Christian Athletes, Youth for Christ, and Christian Camping International. See the resources section for addresses.

Youth Ministries. In addition to your church's youth ministry programs, other ministry opportunities are available to your teenager. In the past several decades, many independent interdenominational Christian youth organizations have sprung up. The oldest and best known of the ones that minister to junior high and high school kids include Youth for Christ/Campus Life, Young Life, and Fellowship of Christian Athletes. The main purpose of these ministries is evangelism, leading kids to Christ. They also offer Bible teaching, Christian fellowship, personal counsel, fun, and recreation. All three emphasize adult leaders building relationships with young people, so each staff member or volunteer is expected to spend many hours each week on the school campus and at school events. Besides weekly club meetings (Campus Life and Young Life) or "Huddles" (FCA), each organization sponsors camps, retreats, trips, and special events and activities.

I worked for twenty-six years on the Campus Life staff of

Youth for Christ, spending countless hours with other parents' teenagers. I know firsthand the value of personal ministry with adolescents. Today, as the parent of two teenagers, I am more convinced than ever of this value. Yet none of the organizations mentioned above has a ministry focused on the high school our Dana attends. Our church has a strong youth group, and Dana has Christian friends, teachers, and counselors in her school, so she is not a spiritual orphan by any means. But I wish we had a campus ministry, with regular visits by caring adults. I wish that a staff member from a solid parachurch organization would relate to Dana the way I related to so many kids in the past.

If you have an effective parachurch youth ministry in your school district, support it and encourage your teenagers to get involved in groups in addition to the one sponsored by your church. Have the youth leaders over for dinner and open your home for meetings; this will help your teenagers become familiar with the leaders and the programs.

In Our Own Lives

The tough choices involve not only exploring the various options for our teenagers to find spiritual nurturing but also examining and committing ourselves to our own spiritual growth. Our teenagers will grow spiritually if we will make the tough choices to model a healthy relationship to God and the church, to teach them spiritual life skills, and to lead them in faith-stretching experiences.

Model. Consider what values you model for your children. What would your teenagers say if someone asked them what value you place on your relationship with God or on church or on the family? What attitude toward the pastor and other church leaders are you projecting?

I know a father who cannot understand why his son has no use for church. Yet this man makes it a regular habit to criticize the church: the sermon "wasn't good"; the soloist "was off key"; the praise songs "were shallow"; the Sunday school teachers "need to be better trained"; and the elders "don't know what they're doing." No wonder the son doesn't have a good picture of church.

We model our values by how we invest our time, money, and emotions. Obviously, some activities take more time than others, so it wouldn't be fair to evaluate people's values simply by how much time they spend on each interest. For example, most people spend from forty to sixty hours a week working and from forty-two to fifty-six hours a week sleeping. These same people may spend only five to ten hours in church services and other church activities, committee meetings, and responsibilities. These statistics do not prove that church is considerably less important to the people than their job and sleep. However, if those people refuse to participate in the life of the church beyond Sunday and often choose to travel on business over the weekend, it would be fair to assume that church isn't very important to them. What about the man who plays golf instead of spending time with his children? How about the woman who loves to spend time with friends but can't spare a minute to listen to her child's description of a day at school? Or what about the person who spends thousands of dollars on a new car or another adult toy but "can't afford" to send a child to camp? Those people preach with their lives that golf, friends, and the car are more important than their children. A person's true values shine through his or her investments.

Throughout Scripture, God tells his people to make their relationship with him the highest priority in their lives: "Hear,

O Israel: The Lord our God, the Lord is one. Love the Lord your God with all your heart and with all your soul and with all your strength. These commandments that I give you today are to be upon your hearts. Impress them on your children. Talk about them when you sit at home and when you walk along the road, when you lie down and when you get up. Tie them as symbols on your hands and bind them on your foreheads. Write them on the doorframes of your houses and on your gates" (Deuteronomy 6:4-9). Clearly, our homes are to be filled with the presence and knowledge of God.

Studies have consistently shown that children pick up the values of their parents. That is, they become most like their parents in how they live and where they invest their lives. Thus, the best way to instill in your teenagers a love for the church is to love the church yourself. This means making worship and Christian education a high priority in your lives, supporting your local church

SPIRITUAL LEADERSHIP

Whatever you do, modern parent, be sure not to force religion down your children's throats. Let them make up their own minds—or so say the pop experts of our time.

The divine Visitor who stopped to see Abraham long ago (Genesis 18:1-4, 16-19) apparently didn't subscribe to such a philosophy. Not that he coerced the young (or old) to serve him whether they liked it or not; after all, the whole notion of giving people a free choice was his to begin with.

But that didn't hinder him from commissioning parents, especially fathers, to "direct" their children and households "to keep the way of the Lord." He fully expected Abraham to take leadership in his home regarding spiritual matters, to set a pace, to let his offspring know that "doing what is right and just" was expected procedure.

There is no way to read this without seeing a proactive role for Abraham.   —Dean Merrill
Wait Quietly: Devotions for a Busy Parent[4]

with your involvement and money, encouraging pastors and other church leaders, and consistently praying for your church.

When I look back on my life, I realize that one of the reasons I have been so heavily involved in local churches throughout my life is the example my parents set. Both were very involved in church, singing in the choir, counseling at camp, serving on a variety of boards and committees, having the pastors and missionaries over for dinner, and participating in small-group Bible studies. I learned from watching my parents that an important expression of my faith in Christ is involvement with a local body of believers.

Model the right values to your children.

Teach. In addition to being good role models, we also should *teach* our children. When considering this responsibility, usually we think of teaching youngsters how to tie their shoes, how to read, and how to perform other useful skills. But we also should teach spiritual life skills, such as how to worship, how to pray, and how to study the Bible.

Teach your children how to worship. Starting when your children are young, help them understand and appreciate each part of the worship services. Work on the unfamiliar songs together. Talk about what the family should give in the offering. Compose a family prayer list that all of you can pray through silently during the prayer time. During the mealtime following a worship service, quiz each other about points and illustrations in the sermon you just heard. After discussing the details of the sermon, ask two simple questions: *So what?* (How does that apply to us?) and *Now what?* (What are we going to do about it?)

When your children approach the teen years, work behind the scenes with Sunday school teachers and pastors. Discuss creative ways to get kids involved in worship services. They can serve as ushers, greeters (looking for visiting kids their own age), and

technical assistants (helping with sound system, lights, projec-
tors, etc.). They can read Scripture, sing, and give personal
testimonies. Being involved in the church services will help give
teenagers ownership and a sense of belonging.

Teach your family how to pray. Do your children know that
prayer is a vital part of your life? What do you pray about as a
family? When I was five years old, my family moved from Chicago
to Rockford, Illinois. I remember my parents explaining that we
should pray about finding a house that would be close to my dad's
work and close to church. We prayed often about that, so I was
thrilled when my mother told me that God had led us to just the
right house. That fact that I can remember that incident about half
a century later testifies to the powerful effect of a godly example.

You can teach the importance of prayer by praying at meals,
before trips, when making major decisions, and during family
devotions. As suggested earlier, you can compose a family prayer
list, consisting of special requests from every member of the
family. Again, starting when your children are young, explain
that prayer is simply talking to God as we would talk to a friend
and that prayers have three main parts: "Thank you" (where we
thank God for who he is and for what he has done), "I'm sorry"
(where we confess our sins to God), and "Please" (where we ask
for God's help). Pray together as a family at mealtimes and
bedtime, making sure that your teenagers have opportunities to
pray often with the family.

Teach your family how to read, study, and apply the Bible.
This can begin by having family devotions. Christian bookstores
offer many excellent resources for devotion time. Memorize
verses together. The *One Year Bible Memory Book for Families*
(Tyndale) is an excellent resource. You may decide to have family
devotions daily, every other day, or once a week. Whatever you

decide, remember that it is important to have a regular time so that everyone knows and can be prepared.

During your family devotional time, teach your children Bible study skills. For a step-by-step approach to use with older kids, see my *How to Apply the Bible* (Tyndale). You can take a passage of Scripture and follow the *People, Place, Plot, Point, Principles, Present, Parallels, Priorities,* and *Plan* steps together. Or use again the two simple questions—*So what?* (How does that apply to us?) and *Now what?* (What are we going to do about it?)—with every passage you read as a family.

One of the most effective ways to get teenagers interested in God's Word is to give them a version of the Bible geared to them. The *Life Application Bible for Students,* for example, includes a reading plan, book introductions, charts, and diagrams. It is filled with Life Application notes, Personality Profiles, Ultimate Issue notes, Moral Dilemma notes, "Here's What I Did" notes, "I Wonder" notes, a Life-Changer Index, and other indexes. Whatever Bible you choose, remember to get one that your teenagers will read and use, not one that you think they should have. I have seen scores of kids carry never-used or hardly opened Bibles to church. Often these Bibles were confirmation or graduation gifts from parents or grandparents. We want our kids to *read* their Bibles, not just carry them.

Teach your children how to worship, pray, and study the Bible.

Stretch. Besides modeling and teaching, you can strengthen and deepen your family's faith through faith-stretching experiences. These can be as simple as monthly visits to a local nursing home or as involved as a missions trip to another country. One family took a short-term missionary trip for a month in the summer. Their children ranged in age from early elementary school to high school, and everyone participated. Their service included helping local missionaries, holding Bible classes, and putting on programs in churches. That may not be feasible for you, but you can find similar opportunities if you look for them.

As previously mentioned, many organizations offer mission trips for teenagers. Although the trips involve raising money and can be risky, they can provide invaluable lessons. Paul Barthwick's book *Youth & Missions* gives many helpful suggestions. See the resources section at the back of this book for further addresses.

Lead your family in faith-stretching experiences.

* * *

It's not unusual for children, especially adolescents, to challenge their parents about attending church and other spiritual activities. Instead of being intimidated by their demands or comparisons with other families, we need to hold the line and make the tough choices—with them and in our own lives.

DON'T MAKE THEM GO
If your teenagers don't want to go to church, don't make them! Instead, every Sunday morning for the next few weeks, while the rest of the family is at church, take them to places like:

1. The burn unit at your local hospital. Visit the kids; read to them; pray over them. These kids would give anything to be at church.

2. The children's cancer ward. These young children are dying. Your kids will wake up to reality and to the fact that they are taking God for granted.

3. A gospel mission. There, families of six to eight people live in a small room, and more than 100 people watch the same television.

Do this in love. Pray for God to change your teenagers' hearts.

—Bill Sanders
youth speaker, author,
and television host of *Straight Talk*

THINK IT THROUGH

1. In what ways have your teenagers expressed a negative attitude about church and spiritual matters?
2. How do you usually respond?
3. What would be a better way to respond?
4. What makes this a tough choice for you?
5. What values do you model to your children in your lifestyle? What would they say are the three most important things in your life?
6. What Christian youth organizations have ministries for your teenagers' school?
7. How will you facilitate and encourage those ministries?
8. What will you do to start or improve your family devotions?
9. What spiritual life skills do you need to teach your children?
10. What is your plan for teaching those skills?
11. What faith-stretching experiences will benefit your family?
12. Which one(s) will you try during the next year?

CHAPTER 4

"Whoever Has the Remote Has the Power"

"Of course they've had their disagreements; all brothers do."
—Ozzie to Harriet
from "Rick's Raise"

"HEY, I WAS watching *Power Pak Pals!*" eight-year-old Brad yells as his high school sister, Kristen, grabs the remote and switches channels.

"Oh, come on!" Kristen yells back. "It's just a rerun. Besides, you know this is the time I always watch *Lovers.*"

"That show is stupid!" offers Brad. "And it's not good anyway. Mom told you that last week."

"Forget it, Brad," she retorts. "I'm watching it, so you'd better get used to it. Why don't you watch television in the basement?"

Suddenly, five-year-old Lisa enters the room and the debate. "Mom says I can watch *Tree House,* so turn to channel 4!"

"Look, Lisa," says Kristen, grasping the remote firmly and holding it up so both her brother and sister can see it clearly, "I have the remote, and I'm watching my program. If Mom wants you to see *Tree House,* use the television in her bedroom!"

"Let's go, Lisa," Brad interjects. "Dad will be home soon anyway, and he will kick Kristen out. The Rattlers game is on in fifteen minutes."

The two kids run from the family room, leaving Kristen on the couch, ready to watch her show alone, but wondering about what her father will do.

The Browns have three television sets—make that four—located in various rooms around the house. Yet with five family members, often an argument flares about what to watch, especially since everyone wants to sit in front of the new big-screen model in the family room. Although they don't live in a large community, the Browns can pull in the city's three network stations and a selection of UHF channels.

Deciding that they needed more channels, however, the Browns recently subscribed to cable. Now their choices seem endless. In fact, some afternoons, right after school, Kristen will surf through the stations, usually hopping among the three music-video channels unless a talk show, soap, or movie catches her attention.

Joe and Elaine Brown liked the idea of having more entertainment and education choices; that's why they got cable. They emphasize *education* when discussing the new television and cable with friends—several channels feature science, history, and other informative programs. But Joe Brown admits that as a sports nut he really enjoys the wide variety of races and games—everything from go-carts to golf, from rugby to wrestling. When Elaine Brown is not at her part-time job, she enjoys some daytime soaps and talk shows. But her favorite programs are the adult situation comedies at night, broadcast after Lisa and Brad have gone to bed.

The Browns really couldn't afford the new television, but considering all the programs they wanted to watch and all the new channels, they thought it was a good investment. Now it stands in the center of the back wall of the family room, just off the kitchen. They can see it from the kitchen table, and sometimes they have it on during dinner.

The Challenge

If asked, the Browns would not admit to watching much television: "Just a few hours a day—more on weekends." Actually, their viewing habits fall right in line with most American families.

In the mid-eighties, families with adolescents had an average of 3.4 television sets.[1] And according to Judith Waldrop, the average two- to five-year-old American child watches about thirty hours of television weekly.[2] "A few hours a day—more on weekends" multiplied by the number of sets translates into anywhere from twenty-five to fifty hours a week. That can add up to several thousand hours a year. Thus, according to Quentin J. Schultze's book *Redeeming Television,* when an average American young person graduates from high school, he or she will have spent about 23,000 hours in front of a television, compared to about 11,000 hours in school. Some estimates are even higher.[3] According to Nielson Media Research, in the years from 1979 to 1980 the average time spent by Americans watching television daily was six hours, thirty-six minutes. By 1988 and 1989, that time had grown to seven hours, two minutes.[4] It's no wonder that by the time children are teenagers, they are hooked on television and are part of the TV generation.

Time Stealer

This television addiction leads to many problems. First, it can be a tremendous waste of time. More than thirty years ago, the chairperson of the Federal Communications Commission, Newton Minow, called television programming a "vast wasteland." Recently, Minow reappeared to announce that the wasteland is worse than ever.[5] These days, viewers are subjected to a steady parade of mindless interviews, inane comedies, empty award shows, sound-bite newscasts, phony docudramas, and twisted soap operas. Often kids (and adults) will simply "watch television," no matter what is on. A typical couch potato plops in front of the television, remote in hand and snacks on the side, and flips from channel to channel. Teenagers who sit and watch television for hours are not exercising, reading, helping others, or getting involved in extracurricular activities. In effect, they are becoming casual and passive observers, consumers, "vidiots," as opposed to active learners and productive members of society. Watching television can waste huge amounts of time.

MIND ROBBER

Too many families let their kids turn television on and keep it on all night long. That competes with reading as well as needed rest. Furthermore, television is an entirely different kind of mental activity than reading. On television, producers and actors do the interpreting. When students read from the printed page, however, they have to interpret. It's excellent mental exercise to read and try to comprehend. It's much less work to have it all digested and presented to you. But everyone wants a quick, easy approach to homework and completion of assignments.

—Sylvia Skarstad
"View from the Chalkboard," *Youthworker*[6]

Values Communicator

Far worse than robbing us of time, television programs model, teach, and preach values that run counter to our Christian faith and family priorities. Consider the following.

Violence. Television shows overflow with assault, rape, abuse, murder, fighting, and war. The *Journal of the American Medical Association* estimates that the average American will have watched 200,000 violent acts and 40,000 slayings on television by age eighteen.[7] The Center for Media and Public Affairs tells us that on any specific day, television viewers can see fourteen violent scenes per hour on HBO, eleven on MTV, ten on CBS, three on ABC, and two on NBC.[8]

Violence is not confined to the evening, adult-entertainment hours. According to George Gerbner, professor of communications at the University of Pennsylvania, every hour of prime-time television contains four violent acts, while every hour of children's programming has thirty-two.[9]

For the last few years, Congress has debated whether violence on television has negatively affected society, especially children. Although no regulative legislation has been forthcoming, three government agencies—the Department of Defense, the U.S. Postal Service, and Amtrak (which together spend almost $70 million annually on television ads)—have decided not to advertise during excessively violent television programs.[10]

Teenage violence is a major problem in America. From the years 1988 to 1993, murders committed by juveniles rose 85 percent. At the annual meeting of the American Association for the Advancement of Science, researchers reported that the country's current homicide epidemic is concentrated among American teenagers. James Alan Fox, dean of the College of Criminal Justice at Northeastern University in Boston, warned: "There are 40 million children in this country under the age of 10. They're growing up young and restless. I'm not optimistic. We'll see a bloodbath in the next 10 years."[11] They can link this rise of violence among our teenagers and the general violent climate in the nation to a number of causes, including guns, drugs, and family disintegration. There is no question, however, that broadcast violence is a major factor. Life is cheap on television.

Some people object to these claims of television's influence on society, explaining that just because people see something done on television doesn't mean that they repeat that act. That certainly is true; people don't mindlessly copy *everything* they see others do. At the same time, however, it is utterly foolish to deny the strong influence of television on our thoughts, lifestyles, values, and buying patterns. That's why advertisers pay millions of dollars for a thirty-second opportunity to tout their products and services. They know the power of the projected image.

Children lean toward violence when they repeatedly see gratuitous blood and gore, crimes with no consequences, corrupt police officers, and violence as a way to settle differences and exact revenge. This message contradicts the Bible's teaching to leave revenge to God (Leviticus 19:18; Romans 12:19) and Jesus' admonitions to be peacemakers (Matthew 5:9), to turn the other cheek (Matthew 5:39), and to "do to others what you would have them do to you" (Matthew 7:12).

Sex. More prevalent than the violence on television is its emphasis on sex. This topic has become an obsession with writers, producers, and directors. One evening during prime time, I turned on the television to check out the lineup of situation comedies. I decided to watch a show until someone on the program made an off-color remark or a sexual innuendo, and then I would switch to another show. Before one half hour had passed, I had watched snippets of four shows. Then I got disgusted and turned off the set.

This sex obsession has moved well beyond sitcoms. Sex holds a prominent place in game shows, mysteries, and late-night talk shows. Yet all these pale in comparison with the daily fare of midday talk shows, tabloid news programs, and daytime dramas. Scenes and stories that would have been banned as pornographic just a few years ago are now accepted as typical viewing. According to a recent report, viewers can expect the following instances of sex per hour on daytime drama: NBC, 4.6; ABC, 7.2; CBS, 7.7.[12] And the topics and discussion on talk shows hosted by Jenny Jones, Geraldo Rivera, Phil Donahue, Jerry Springer, and others feature every kind of sexual aberration.

Most frustrating are the programs produced and marketed specifically for young people. Many contain sexually explicit scenes, story lines, references, and humor. These shows include *Beverly Hills 90210, Baywatch, Melrose Place, Saturday Night Live,* shows on MTV, and others. Teenagers feel pressured to watch these shows because they hear their friends talking about them at school, and they don't want to feel left out.

MTV

In my fifteen years of working with young people, speaking to more than 250,000 each year in school assemblies, answering thousands of letters each year, interviewing hundreds of troubled teens each year preparing for my talk show *Straight Talk,* and having written fourteen books, I have found MTV to be the single most damaging influence on young people. If your kids watch MTV, you will find it almost impossible to teach them right from wrong or even to read the Bible with them! MTV promotes Satanism, homosexuality, bestiality, racism, sexual promiscuity, violence, crime, rape, and murder. MTV won't allow even one song that promotes sexual abstinence. MTV founder Bob Pittman said, "We own America's fourteen-year-olds."

—Bill Sanders
youth speaker, author, and
television host of *Straight Talk*

Sometimes television advertisements can be as bad as some of the programs. Perfume, jeans, automobiles, deodorant, and a host of other products use sex to sell. Again, some ads for underwear and aftershave lotion are extremely suggestive and would have been considered pornographic just a few years ago.

Television regularly portrays premarital sex as natural and desirable, adultery as inevitable and normal, homosexuality as a viable lifestyle option, and marital commitment as passé. These emphases directly oppose God's commands prohibiting adultery (Exodus 20:14), lust (Exodus 20:17; Proverbs 6:25), homosexual sex (Romans 1:27; 1 Corinthians 5:9), and sexual promiscuity (Proverbs 7:4-27; 1 Corinthians 5:9-11; 6:18-20; Colossians 3:5). These cultural views of sex also oppose the strong biblical teaching of the sanctity of marriage (Jeremiah 29:6; Malachi 2:14-16; Matthew 19:3-9; Romans 7:2; 1 Corinthians 7:8-14; Hebrews 13:4).

Materialism. Another, more subtle, message presented on

the tube involves money, power, and possessions. The "beautiful people" live in mansions, drive expensive automobiles, fly all over the world, live royally, and purchase whatever they want. Celebrities parade across the screen, accepting Emmys, Oscars, Golden Globes, Grammys, and other awards. Stars are featured on talk shows, game shows, and the news and are interviewed at premieres, backstage, and after athletic contests. Children look up to these stars, seek to emulate them, and dream of someday having what they have.

UNDERSTANDING THE POWER

I've noticed that parents don't know youth culture very well. So I tell them to watch television. They will see that sex is featured on almost every television show and in every movie. I also encourage them to buy a *Seventeen* magazine and check out the stories and the ads. Our teenagers are being sold values and morals that certainly aren't Christian.
                                                        —David Olshine
                                                Director of Youth Ministry,
                                        Columbia International University

Many other programs also appeal to the lust for money and power. Again we can't overlook the ads, most of which promote conspicuous consumption. Today we have info-mercials and shopping networks that make it even easier to buy what we don't need. Also most states now have legalized gambling, an industry that advertises often on television.

The main message seems to be that money equals happiness. Contrast this with Jesus' words of warning, "No servant can serve two masters. Either he will hate the one and love the other, or he will be devoted to the one and despise the other. You cannot serve both God and Money" (Luke 16:13) and Paul's admonition, "For the love of money is a root of all kinds of evil. Some people, eager for money, have wandered from the faith and pierced themselves with many griefs" (1 Timothy 6:10). Also, Hebrews reminds us, "Keep your lives free from the love of money and be content with what you have, because God has said, 'Never will I leave you; never will I forsake you'" (Hebrews 13:5).

Values That Undermine Family's Values. Television programs portray many other lifestyles and values that undermine our homes and our parenting efforts. Just the fact that complex problems in families, between friends, and in society are solved in sixty minutes or less presents a false and very idealistic view of life. And God is never part of the solution. Also, most of these broadcast solutions are *politically correct;* that is, they fall in line with the prevailing notion of individualism and tolerance of anyone except evangelical Christians. For example:

- A girl wonders if she should sleep with her boyfriend; she knows that her parents would object. A close friend advises her that it's fine if she really loves him and if he uses a condom. It's her choice.
- A Bible-quoting, neighbor-judging father is discovered to be a drug kingpin. The free-spirited, promiscuous, single mom next door counsels the man's suicidal wife.
- A talk-show host interviews a film star who has been arrested for visiting a prostitute. The two men pass off the incident with flippant comments like, "It's really nothing. Any male would have done the same thing. What's the big deal?"
- Undercover detectives reveal that a conservative preacher is the secret leader of an anti-government, paramilitary group. In addition, he has molested

several girls in his congregation. A relieved town
thanks God when the preacher's duplicity is uncovered.
- A rising star in the advertising world discovers that she
is pregnant. Close friends and coworkers advise her not
to tell her husband and to have an abortion because
having the baby would "complicate her life" and force
her to abandon her career.

Many situation comedies portray parents, especially fathers, as weird, out of touch, and generally confused. Often the children must counsel their parents on the right course of action to take. And in most televised relationships, *commitment* is a dirty word; struggling spouses are encouraged to leave if they are no longer "in love" or are not realizing their potential.

At the pinnacle of television values stand individual happiness and fulfillment. That end seems to justify almost any means. There's no telling what perversion or negative value television will promote next.

Television can undermine our families' values and faith.

COMMAND CENTER

We are by now well into a second generation of children for whom television has been their first and most accessible teacher and, for many, their most reliable companion and friend. There is no audience so young that it is barred from television. There is no education so exalted that it is not modified by television. And most important of all, there is no subject of public interest—politics, news, education, religion, science, sports—that does not find its way to television. Which means that all public understanding of these subjects is shaped by the biases of television.

—Neil Postman
Amusing Ourselves to Death[13]

* * *

At this point, it may seem as if I have portrayed television as a monster that spews nothing but lies, filth, and corruption into our homes. On balance I must add that we can find many fine television networks and programs. Unfortunately, however, positive programming is increasingly becoming the exception, not the rule.

The Conflict

The values portrayed on television can affect our families and disrupt our homes. The sad thing is, many parents contribute to their teenagers' excessive television viewing by their own undisciplined lifestyles. Many parents are the root of the problems television brings into their homes.

Some families have a television in just about every room. In some families the kids have their own televisions, a small one sits under the cupboards in the kitchen, and another perches in the van. It always seems as if at least one set is broadcasting somewhere in the house. In fact, often the first thing some parents do when they enter a room is turn on the television set.

Whatever the reason, many people find it difficult to turn off their sets, even when they are talking with a friend in a home or on the phone. Many times I have tried to carry on a conversation with someone while his or her television was blaring in the same room. It was virtually impossible. Besides having to talk over the sound of the set, our attention was constantly drawn to whatever was on the screen. Even a slow-paced and relaxing professional golf tournament turned our heads and caused our minds to wander. In many homes, the television stays on after everyone has left the room, providing background noise when no one is watching.

ELECTRONIC INVADER

There's a house in my neighborhood that stands as a late-night monument to the place of television in American culture. Night after night, the eerie blue glow of the television provides the only visible illumination in the house. For many men, women, and children, TV has taken its place as an illuminator, clarifying and explaining life. . . .

Like popular music, television's ability to define reality and guide children and teens through life has increased over time in proportion to the decreasing influence of the family, school, and church. Parental influences deteriorate when parents are absent from the home or oblivious to what their children and teens are watching. These children learn about life and the outside world from someone other than Mom or Dad. All too often, that someone is the electronic baby-sitter. As long as they have the ability to turn on the TV and operate the remote, children of all ages have unlimited access to television's good and bad, including information and programming that is often unsuitable for adults.

—Walt Mueller
Understanding Today's Youth Culture[14]

Television holds such an important place in some homes that it sits prominently in the family room, the center attraction, with all the chairs and couches facing it. Some parents use television almost as a baby-sitter. They sit their babies and toddlers in front of the television, hoping that the sounds and images will fascinate the children and keep them quiet. These parents find it easy, then, to continue to use television this way, with older children watching kids' shows and cartoons. As the process continues, the whole family becomes hooked, addicted to television. Many parents admit that the family comes together only when they sit and watch certain shows.

We shouldn't be surprised at the pull of television and the addiction. Television producers are experts at projecting images that capture our attention, tantalize us, and pull us in. If you want to see the epitome of this expertise, watch the ads during the Super Bowl, where airtime costs about a million dollars a minute. Advertisers know that they have to pack those seconds with fascinating images, up-tempo music, and memorable sound bites in order to get their messages across. And each ad is loaded with creativity. We may complain about all the ads on television, but we watch them—and we buy. Also, individual programs get our attention and tweak our curiosity by teasing us with fascinating promotional ads. Then they keep us watching a specific show by using intriguing stories that continue from week to week. Whether it's a daytime soap opera or a prime-time dramatic series, we just have to see what happened to Luke or Chad or Nicole or the conniving Erica. (And who shot J. R. anyway?)

With television viewing ingrained in our lifestyles, we can easily overlook many of its shortcomings and negative messages. Or the poor programming can wear us down, inoculating us against any sense of moral outrage. For example, because words such as *damn, hell,* and *my God* are sprinkled throughout most television scripts, we hardly notice them anymore. The same is true of partial nudity, adultery, and violence. Remember when a *husband and wife* couldn't be seen in the same bed together? That may have been a little conservative, but now, at the other extreme, anyone and everyone can jump into bed, wearing anything or nothing, leaving very little to the imagination about what they are doing. But we have become so worn down, so used to those lifestyles, that very little shocks us anymore.

Cable television and satellite dishes bring a smorgasbord of networks and shows. This wide array appeals to many parents because they want more options from which to choose or because they want certain narrow-focus, specialized channels available only this way. But the dish or cable introduces many bad options

TV NEEDS MOUTH WASHED OUT WITH SOAP

Someone who makes a living in part by counting naughty words on TV has confirmed what anyone who watches the tube already knows: The airwaves are becoming more crowded with obscenities, profanity, and toilet talk.

Actually, you can put a number on it. . . . Southern Illinois University professor Barbara Kaye found that the airwaves were 45% more polluted in 1995 than they were in 1990. There are more references to excretion and body parts, sex acts and reproductive organs on commercial, over-the-air TV than ever.

Maybe it's ratings. Or maybe it's an adolescent urge to be clever. Usually it's rationalized as a reflection of "reality." And mostly, it's out of place.

This is no call for censorship. It is, however, a call for common sense and civility. . . . Adults who yearn for a break from the constant and growing assault of polluted language—at work, at school, in stores, on the bus and L, and on the sidewalk—deserve a break. And parents who want to preserve their children's right to have a childhood deserve a refuge.

—Dennis A. Britton
editorial, *Chicago Sun-Times*[15]

along with the good. MTV, for example, is included in the basic package of most cable companies. Then, if parents don't want their children watching certain channels or programs (on purpose or by accident), they have to monitor all the viewing or have the channels blocked, often at an additional cost.

So, What's a Parent to Do?

What are our choices as we guide our teenagers' viewing habits? Do we wring our hands and feel helpless? Do we pretend that television is harmless and that it won't negatively affect our teenagers? Do we nag? Do we force our teenagers to watch only certain programs? Do we set the pace by watching anything and everything?

Let me suggest that we have several positive options. They may not be easy choices, but they will lead to a healthy home.

The Choice

Most houses have doors and locks to keep out animals and unwelcome humans. To keep their homes clean, most home-owners place mats at the entrances for wiping feet and insist that people remove their muddy shoes before entering. And most parents protect their children from insidious strangers and other threats to physical and emotional health. Thus, it seems strange for Christian moms and dads to open their homes to intruders who would undermine their values, harm their children, and even destroy their families. But that happens when we allow unregulated television to invade our lives and monopolize our time.

The news about television is not all bad. We can use television, a marvelous electronic appliance, to inform, educate, and enter-tain. But we must control its use, and that will take tough choices.

Just Say No!

The easiest way to control the television is to eliminate it entirely from the house. Some parents have taken that drastic step. They have found that life without television forces them to use their creativity for in-house entertainment. Puzzles, books, games, and music fill the void. No television also means fewer distractions and more time to read, do homework, play, and discuss.

This will be a radical move, so you may want to have a trial run first. Challenge the family to go for a month without televi-sion—a television fast. Then offer several creative options to television viewing. At first, family members will experience withdrawal. But after a while they will get used to it and perhaps even see the benefits of life without television. After a month, you can decide whether to extend the fast, to return to the old habits, or to go all the way and remove all the sets.

Banning television entirely may have a downside or two. If young children have never seen a television set, they won't know what they are missing for a few years. But it is virtually impossible to keep them from television entirely. When they play at a friend's house, they will be exposed to television programs. As they get older, they will become increasingly aware of television and the absence of a television in their own home. Television sets are virtually everywhere: school and church classrooms, restaurants, airport lounges, hospital waiting rooms, stores, malls, doctors' offices, amusement parks, buses, and planes. Seeing all those sets can raise your kids' curiosity level and build a thirst for television. You may find that your children get a television entertainment fix at a friend's house. If that is the case, you will need to work hard at teaching your kids to be discerning in what they watch.

Another problem may occur if you suddenly remove television from kids who are used to it. They may rebel and purposely watch shows elsewhere, just to assert their independence. That's why it is important to make this a family decision, if possible, when your kids are older.

Just Say Whoa!

If you don't remove the televisions altogether, then you should definitely limit the family's viewing, including your own. Even if your family is hooked on the tube and has already developed terrible viewing habits, it's not too late to change. Again, you may want to begin the process with the television fast described above. Then, at the end of the month, call a family meeting, discuss the experience, and decide on new viewing rules. The rules could include:

- Homework must be done before the television is turned on.
- No one can just "watch television." Instead, each person must have specific programs in mind and submit a list of viewing choices that will be cleared each week (or month) by the "viewing board" (one parent and one child, with rotating membership each month).
- Parents have the right to veto any program because of content.
- If more than one desired show is on at the same time, family members will take turns watching the television set of their choice. The others will have to use the other sets.
- If someone is already reading, studying, or listening to music in a room, the other family members will watch television in another room.

Be sure to explain the rationale for these rules. Begin with the biblical principles of seeking God first (Matthew 6:33), glorifying God with our lives (1 Corinthians 10:31), making wise use of our time (Ephesians 5:15-16), filling our minds with what is wholesome and good (Philippians 4:8), avoiding love for the world (1 John 2:15-17), and respecting each other (1 Corinthians 13:4-7; Ephesians 4:32). Then share your feelings about what it means to be a parent—it's a wonderful, God-given responsibility, but it's not easy—and that you want to be the best parent possible.

Monitor not only the amount of television watched but also the content of specific programs. Some families use daily limits, while others assign a specific amount of time for each family member per week. A simple chart can track the viewing time and choices. Subject everyone to this system. You can vary the hours on weekends and holidays, for school assignments, and for special circumstances; you may even want to add programs that the family watches together. But try to stick with a set schedule for a while so that exceptions don't become the rule. Also, lean to the conservative side when you start. It will be much easier to expand the number of hours than to reduce them later.

When you judge the content of the programs, you will find it easy to evaluate shows on both ends of the spectrum. You will approve of some programs almost immediately because you have seen them and know they are good. You will find it fairly easy to disapprove of programs at the other end of the spectrum.

THE 23RD CHANNEL

The TV is my shepherd
I shall not want.
It makes me lie down on the sofa.
It leads me away from the faith.
It destroys my soul.
It leads me in the path of sex and violence for the sponsor's sake.
Yea, though I walk in the shadow of Christian responsibilities, there
    will be no interruption, for the TV is with me.
Its cable and remote control, they comfort me.
It prepares a commercial for me in the presence of my worldliness.
It anoints my head with humanism and consumerism.
My coveting runneth over.
Surely laziness and ignorance shall follow me all the days of my life,
    and I shall dwell in the house, watching TV forever.

—*Daily Guideposts*

The programs in the middle—either they have borderline content or you haven't seen them—will be much more difficult. To be fair and to minimize disagreements, allow your teens to watch the program in question *with you.* Afterward, talk it over; be honest about your feelings and thoughts, and listen respectfully to your son or daughter. Then make your decision and hold to it.

If, after viewing and discussing the show with your teen, you see the program as on the border of being questionable, put the program on probation. That is, let your teenagers know that if the sex, violence, off-color jokes, and negative values occur regularly, the show will be placed in the unapproved category.

Obviously you won't be able to avoid all controversy—even the best referees, umpires, and judges are questioned. But you will be fair. It will help if you and your spouse open yourselves to the same judgment. In other words, allow your teenagers to question the merits of the shows you watch on the same grounds.

Limit the amount of television the family watches, and allow only approved shows in the house. Then fill the time with play and creative interaction. Build family time into the schedule.

Just Say Grow!

Remember this important principle: Use television; don't let television use you. Use the TV for entertainment, education, spiritual development, discussion, and family growth.

Watch Good Programs. The most obvious way to use television is to watch the right programs. Just as the daily schedule contains many rotten options, it also presents many positive, wholesome shows. Talk with parents and pastors at church to see which ones they recommend. There is no guarantee that the values of these parents will exactly match yours, but it is a good place to start.

For education, check out public television and The Discovery Channel, Arts & Entertainment, and other cable options. And look for specials about historical or contemporary events that are occasionally shown on the major networks.

For Christian growth, tune into the Christian channel in your city. Look for shows not only that will help you but also that the whole family will enjoy. For example, Bill Sanders' show *Straight Talk,* a syndicated program for teenagers, is an excellent choice.

Any number of shows can stimulate discussion among family members: a news story, an investigative report, a family situation comedy, a made-for-television drama. At times, teachers will give students the assignment of watching a specific program. Watch the show with your teenagers and discuss it afterward.

For pure entertainment, look for programs that the whole family will enjoy. A few years ago, *The Cosby Show* topped the ratings week after week. Completely clean and supportive of family values, the program pictured real life in a humorous way. Families could laugh and learn together as they watched. Granted, few shows like that exist, but you can find them buried in the schedule. Some of the most entertaining and thought-provoking programs are reruns.

Use a VCR. Even if you don't use your set for watching television programs, you can use it as an excellent source for entertainment and education by using it with a videocassette player. You can rent and watch good, positive videos with no commercial interruptions. In most video rental stores, you can find treasures hidden among the hundreds of tapes offered for rental or sale. The best bets include oldies or current G-rated films and animated features. Talk with Christian friends about their favorites, and consult newsletters that describe and evaluate movies and videos. See the resources section at the end of this book for helpful guides to wholesome videos.

Christian companies have jumped into video production in a big way. At first, most of the videos were for children, including several animated series. In the last few years, however, early adolescents have been the target audience. Some of the best videos are produced and distributed by Tyndale House Publishers, Focus on the Family, Word Publishing, Gospel Films, and Broadman & Holman. Most Christian bookstores have a good selection. Some church libraries invest in videos and then "rent" them for a dollar or two a week.

You may want to choose an age-specific video for a certain child to watch alone. You could rent a video that will serve to start a discussion with one child or with the family. Or you could make a huge bowl of popcorn and watch a video together as a whole family just for fun. Videos can provide hours of controlled, wholesome entertainment and stimulation for personal growth.

Discuss What You See. Television shows and videos can provide many opportunities for meaningful discussion. As you watch, look for scenes, dialogue, and themes that you can talk about afterward or that you can use as illustrations during dinner discussions. Don't do this with every program, or your kids will think you want only to teach and lecture—timing is very important. But you and your family can learn from each other as you interact with what you see on the tube.

- If a situation comedy centers on an embarrassing teen-age situation, you can ask when your kids have felt like that and how they responded.
- If a dramatic show features an interpersonal conflict, you can discuss the biblical way to resolve that conflict.
- When a newscast highlights a personal tragedy or struggling family, you can lead your family in prayer for those hurting people.
- If a Christmas special focuses only on secular holiday celebrations, you can talk about how the special ignored Christ.
- If a story resolves a complex and difficult problem in less than an hour, you can give your insights and discuss a more realistic approach to that problem.
- When a show highlights and promotes lifestyles and values contrary to what God desires, you can discuss the media's subtle influence on kids and families and why it is difficult to live for Christ in contemporary society.

Look for opportunities to teach. Use television as an effective discussion starter.

Talk Back. Negative values that demean our families and our Christian faith can suddenly appear on almost any show, even those that are usually positive and family oriented. If it is not feasible to discuss this problem later with your teenagers, talk back to the television set right then, refuting the lies and setting the record straight. The commercial break may provide the best time for this.

Speaking of commercials, often the advertisements are the worst offenders. As mentioned earlier in this chapter, advertisers know what sells products. Professional and expert, they use whatever it takes to get their messages across and spur sales. Teach your kids how to analyze the ads, to cut through the baloney, and to see through the smoke. Laugh at the ridiculous claims and implied benefits of certain products, especially when competing companies make the same unbelievable statements.

Will using a certain brand of toothpaste really enhance one's sex appeal? Will wearing a pair of athletic shoes really help a person jump higher and run faster? Will eating a certain brand of cereal really make someone grow into a world-class athlete? Will using the right deodorant guarantee an outstanding business presentation? Of course not! Yet we watch those ads over and over, and subconsciously we begin to believe their outrageous claims.

The most popular ads seem to use the following techniques:

Image. The entire commercial features fantastic images and great music, a humorous interchange, or a dramatic vignette, with the company's logo appearing at the end. The ad mentions nothing about the product, makes no claims, and highlights no important characteristics. Instead, it pictures fun, excitement, happiness, or success, implying that the highlighted company and its products will lead to one of those positive results.

Humor. Whether the commercial features professional athletes joking around with each other, situations where everything goes wrong, or weird salespeople, these ads get us laughing at the actors or at the competition and say little or nothing about the product. After the thirty-second spot, we feel good about the company. Some of the most effective commercials use babies, small children, or animals.

Extremity. These creative advertisements stretch the imagination. We know they aren't true, but they capture our attention and are fun to watch. Trips to outer space, flying cars, ski-jumping

TEEN DEVOTION

Movies, records, radio, and television occupy a huge place in the lives of teenagers. They spend an extraordinary amount of time and energy selecting and consuming their art diet ("devouring" may be a more accurate word). A recent Gallup survey showed that teenagers' favorite pastimes are going out with friends, watching television, and going to movies. Entertainment impresarios know well this teen devotion to popular art—mass-produced entertainment disseminated through the media—and work hard to expand pop art's already major role in youth culture. To do so, the industry directs its attention to adolescents' primary psychological needs for identity, intimacy, and meaning.

—Quentin J. Schultze
Dancing in the Dark[16]

recliners, skydiving celebrities, talking animals, fast cars, and fantastic contests—anything is possible with these ads. We learn very little about the featured product, but the image is imbedded in our minds.

Endorsements. These ads use celebrities, usually professional athletes, to hawk the wares. A popular coach promotes a department-store chain; a superstar quarterback sells gloves; an all-star center explains what tires to buy; a former tennis champion endorses aspirin; a television celebrity extols the benefits of a phone company; a gaggle of former pros push beer. The idea behind this approach is, "If it's good enough for [the celebrity], then it's good enough for me!"

Sex. Probably the most common advertising enticement, sex is used to sell almost anything. Curvaceous models slide their bodies alongside any number of products and offer them to us: wine coolers, automobiles, aftershave lotion, shopping centers, pet food, and on and on. And often the ads feature men and women together, by a pool, on a beach, in a shower, at a resort, and in bed. Lustful imagination gets our attention, pulls us into the ads, and keeps us watching.

Fantastic Claims. For many years, advertisers could say almost anything they wanted about their products. When the Federal Communications Commission began to enforce truth in advertising, companies had to alter their approach and be more subtle with their claims. Riding the edge or adhering to the *letter* of the law, television commercials continue to imply amazing, nearly miraculous, results: weight loss without work, freedom from debt, effortless meal preparation, affordable luxury, happiness, leisure, fun, success!

Use these ads as discussion starters. Talk about the implications and the subtle lies. Ask about the advertising approach and why people may want to buy the product. Analyze the ads from a biblical perspective. Laugh at the ridiculous claims. Boycott the offending companies.

Don't be afraid to talk back to the television. The set can't hear you, but your kids can.

* * *

Television plays a major role in our society, entertaining, informing, molding public opinion, promoting lifestyles, and shaping values. Instead of allowing this electronic intruder to use you and your family, allowing images of violence, sex, materialism, and anti-Christian values to undermine your home, use television to teach and to build your family in the faith. Watch what *you* watch, restrict your viewing, choose good shows, use a VCR, discuss what you see, and talk back to the television.

THINK IT THROUGH

1. During a typical week, how much time does each member of your family spend in front of a television?
2. What do you appreciate and enjoy about television?
3. What bothers you about television? What do you dislike about this medium?
4. In what ways is television affecting you and your family positively?
5. What effects of television do you see on your teenagers?
6. How do your teenagers respond to your input about television viewing?
7. What negative effects of television do you see on you and your family?
8. What will you do in the next couple of weeks to change your family's television viewing habits?
9. Why will this be a tough choice?
10. How will you involve your teenagers in the decision-making process?
11. What will you do to determine which shows are good and which are bad?
12. What positive and helpful television shows do you want your family to watch?
13. What television shows do you want to eliminate from your home?
14. How will you use television to help your family grow?

CHAPTER 5

"Pump Up the Volume"

"Well, I wouldn't make too many suggestions, dear. Maybe a lot of things have changed since you had a band."
—Harriet to Ozzie

"Well, sure, but the basic principles of dance music never change."
—Ozzie to Harriet
from "Rick, the Drummer"

BOOM, BOPPA, BOOM! Suddenly dishes rattle in the kitchen cupboards, and the family room wall shakes. Jumping out of his chair, Robert Alexander walks quickly to the hallway and yells, "Justin, turn that thing down. It's too loud!" With no response and the bass continuing to reverberate throughout the house, Robert walks down the hallway and bursts into his son's room. There sits twelve-year-old Justin, on the floor between the speakers, back to the door, studying for his science test.

"Justin!" his dad exclaims, "I told you to turn down that stuff. It's way too loud. Pretty soon the neighbors will be complaining."

"What?" Justin answers, looking up from his book. Then reaching over to the radio, he turns the volume down a notch and then continues, "I'm sorry, Dad, what did you say?"

"Obviously you couldn't hear me because the music was too loud," replies Justin's dad. "I've been trying to tell you for a while to turn it down. It's shaking the whole house. Besides, how can you study with all that noise?"

"I always study while listening to music. It helps me relax," answers Justin.

"Relax? You've got to be kidding!" his dad scoffs and then asks: "What group is that anyway? I don't think I've heard them before. That's pretty hard stuff."

"Insidious Squash," answers Justin. "I want to buy their new CD, *Gotta Gotta Getcha*. It's boss!"

Shaking his head, his dad adds, "Well, just keep it down. Other people live here besides you." Then, closing the door behind him, he goes back down the hall to the family room and tries to resume reading the paper.

Later, when Justin comes out for dinner, he wears his headphones and moves to rhythm only he can hear. Then, turning off his Walkman, he takes his place at the table, next to his younger sister, Shayleen. His dad asks: "Now what are you listening to? That Squash group again?"

"No. It's another hot group—Killa U. It's great rap! I borrowed the tape from Carlos," answers Justin before diving into his meal.

His mom interjects, "Well, just don't listen during our meal. This is family time."

After dinner, Justin's mom drives him to the mall to buy a shirt for the school choir. During the entire fifteen-minute trip Justin searches the radio, changing stations continually, but listening the most to Z-91 ("all rock, all the time") with disc jockey Dirty Dan. In addition to snippets of several artists, he hears Insidious Squash and Killa U again. And he stumbles onto HangNail, another popular singer. "All right!" Justin exclaims. "Is that guy totally cool or what?"

Later, as Robert and Carol Alexander discuss the day's events, Carol asks, "What was that all about with Justin this evening?"

"It's his music again," answers Robert. "Lately that seems to be all he cares about. I sure don't pretend to understand it. What kind of a name is Insidious Squash anyway? And 'Kill-some-thing-or-other'? It's beyond me!"

"I know what you mean," Carol responds. "On the way to the mall, Justin kept changing radio stations until he would find a song he liked. And you should hear Dirty Dan on Z-91. I know where he got his name! This rock and rap and other stuff sounds pretty bad, especially the words—when I can understand them. Should we let Justin listen to that junk? He never used to be like this, but lately he always has to have the radio or stereo turned on and turned up."

"I don't know, honey," replies Robert. "But remember, we had our hits too. And *our* parents didn't understand those groups either. The music didn't hurt us, so maybe we should just ignore the situation—as long as Justin keeps it turned town a bit and his grades don't suffer."

The discussion continues for another half hour, with Robert and Carol Alexander questioning their parenting skills, the direction their son is headed, and his effect on the younger children. They also wonder what other parents think of them or if other parents have similar struggles.

Robert Alexander makes a good point: for decades, music has stood between parents and their adolescent children as a source of misunderstanding and conflict. In fact, nowhere is the generation gap more obvious than with the teenagers' entertainment choices. And nothing seems to identify the younger generation more than their music.

The Challenge

Beginning as early as fifth grade, children start listening regularly to popular music, tuning in the rock station and buying the latest hits. They may learn about the music through an older sibling or television, but friends exert the strongest influence. Early adolescents like to act older, so they try to dress like older kids, talk like them, and listen to their music.

A Social Phenomenon

It is important to understand that children gravitate to teenage music, radio stations, videos, and movies primarily for social reasons. In fact, most kids do not begin by *liking* the music itself, especially those whose parents don't listen regularly to party metal, rap, alternative, or the latest musical fad. Thus, parents become very confused when the older child begins to listen; they wonder where their son or daughter got that desire and why he or she has changed so much.

My wife, Gail, and I first experienced this with our daughter Kara. In fifth grade, she began listening to rock radio stations, and she wanted to dress up like a "punk rocker" for Halloween. We were mystified because we knew we had not exposed her to that type of music at home. Parents of Kara's friends expressed similar questions and frustrations. I remember two fathers in particular. These men were not especially religious or conservative in their lifestyles, yet both, at different times, complained to me about "the music these kids listen to," the "dirty disc jockeys," and the "junk" in PG and PG-13 movies. Parents voice legitimate concerns, but kids tune in to the junk because that's what everyone at school seems to be listening to and watching.

We must remember that kids are social creatures; they want to be like their friends and to belong to the crowd. Also, music symbolizes growing up, especially songs that feature adult themes. Eventually many teens move beyond focusing on what's currently "in" as they broaden their tastes and learn to appreciate a wide variety of musical styles. These days Kara (now in college), for example, also enjoys some oldies like the songs of the Carpenters, a couple of groups reminiscent of the folk music of the sixties, contemporary Christian rock, and even country.

Entertainment Is a Pervasive Force

I remember going through this stage of being fascinated by popular music. As a young teenager during the era of Elvis Presley, Ricky Nelson, Pat Boone, Connie Francis, Fats Domino, Buddy Holly, and Bill Haley and the Comets, I listened to the rock-and-roll disc jockeys on the radio (at that time a new phenomenon in American culture) and bought the records.

Although my parents didn't say much about my identification with the popular crowd, I'm sure they were as concerned as parents are today, especially after seeing Elvis shake his pelvis on the *Ed Sullivan Show*. Yet those artists and their offerings were innocent and tame compared with contemporary fare. Bob DeMoss, youth culture specialist for Focus on the Family, states: "Things are *not* the same today as they were when Elvis sang 'You Ain't Nothin' But a Hound Dog'; kids are plugged into their music in a very personal way; and that music has the power to influence the human spirit for good or for evil." [1] And today, popular music is a 6.25 billion-dollar-per-year industry, with its influence felt in every area of life.

These days, popular musicians sing and rap violent, profane, and obscene lyrics. I wouldn't dare reprint the words of the offending songs for fear of repulsing most readers. You can see Tipper Gore's book *Raising PG Kids in an X-rated Society*, Walt Mueller's *Understanding Today's Youth Culture*, and DeMoss's *Learn to Discern* for a thorough analysis. Let me just say that you probably cannot imagine more degraded and twisted messages—I am not exaggerating! In addition, disc jockeys on the teenage radio stations play many of these songs, promote others that are too obscene to play on the air, and fill the airways with double entendres and sexually explicit segues. Radio stations now regularly broadcast profanity and suggestive humor that would have been censored when our children were very young.

In addition to the music, consider movies and videos. Each year, the content quality slips lower and lower, with the latest productions featuring violence, irreverence, and every sort of sexual activity and perversion. Michael Medved, movie critic and cohost of *Sneak Previews* on PBS, states: "Hollywood's crisis is, at its very core, a crisis of values. It's not 'mediocrity and escapism' that leave audiences cold, but sleaze and self-indulgence. What troubles people about the popular culture isn't the competence with which it's shaped, but the messages it sends, the view of the world it transmits. Hollywood no longer reflects—or even respects—the values of most American families. On many of the important issues in contemporary life, popular entertainment seems to go out of its way to challenge conventional notions of decency."[2] Making matters worse, the movie rating system has become virtually meaningless, and most newspaper and television reviews focus on the production and acting quality and ignore the content. The only way for a parent to know of a movie's acceptability is to see it.

CIVIL WAR
In my estimation, the powerful voices of the American youth culture that we're studying—advertising, television, and music—form one of the primary battlegrounds of this civil war of values.
—Robert G. DeMoss Jr.
Learn to Discern[3]

Perhaps the most dramatic change in the past several years has been the home video revolution. For a few dollars and a videocassette player attached to a television set, a person can watch just about anything that he or she wants, in the privacy of the home. Movies that only a few years ago would have been rated R, or even X, are now being rented and seen by children of all ages. Video rentals and sales comprise a gigantic business. Every week new videos are made available through the mail, video rental stores in just about every strip mall, grocery stores, and even some fast-food restaurants.

Music videos combine these two very popular entertainment media. Popularized through Music Television (MTV), Video Hits-1 (VH-1), other cable channels, and some network programming, music videos have captured the attention of the younger generation. Now, at the push of a button, kids can have their own private concerts with their favorite artists. Not only can they hear the music, they also can *see* the artists perform along with a dazzling array of dramatic visual images that follow the rhythm and underscore the words. Music videos often reinforce and magnify obscene, occultish, and violent lyrics through the projected images and antics. In the past, a complaint about rock music was that the words were unintelligible. Today we can *see* what the words mean, and very little is left to the imagination. In addition to sexual activity and perversion, many rap musicians and others promote rape, drug and alcohol abuse, satanism, suicide, and murder through their performances.

THE VIDEO FACTOR

When I began working with high school students in the late sixties and early seventies, kids were into popular music in a big way, as they still are today. Some of the rock groups promoted drug use and antisocial behavior through their lyrics, lifestyles, and antics on stage. But the influence of these performers was limited to their recordings and occasional appearances on television or in a live concert. Today, however, through MTV, VH-1, and videos, these groups can have almost instant influence as kids see and hear them over and over. I have seen the effects of this phenomenon first in fashion, as kids emulated their favorite entertainers' clothing and hairstyles, and then in language and lifestyle.

—David Veerman
Parenting Passages[4]

Entertainment Is a Powerful Influence

It's bad enough to be assaulted by obscenity and pornography. The images can fill the mind and linger for days. Far worse, however, is the fact that people often live out what they see; their behavior changes. And far more damaging than nude scenes and vulgarity are the values and lifestyles portrayed in television shows, movies, and videos. In movie plots, most of the sex occurs *outside* of marriage. Religious people, especially evangelical Christians, are portrayed as uneducated dupes or dangerous con artists. Pleasure is pictured as the highest good, which should be pursued constantly, regardless of the cost to family, friends, or employer. Life is cheap.

Thus, with the popularity and ready availability of raunchy and anti-Christian entertainment, our kids can't help but be affected by what they hear and see. Music, movies, and videos exert tremendous influence on young people through the following means:

The message. Advertisers spend millions of dollars to convince potential customers to buy their products. These savvy marketers realize that a message set to music and accompanied by striking visual images will motivate listeners and viewers to spend their money. Now consider teenagers who hear a popular singer croon, "I want your sex," "Let's make love," or another sexually suggestive lyric. As with an advertising jingle, the words sink in. The same is true with performers who urge occult practices, drug usage, or violence. Kids get the message.

Celebrity endorsements. Another effective advertising technique involves celebrities who link their name, face, fame, and reputation with a product. This lends credibility to the advertiser's claims and encourages those who want to identify with the endorsing celebrity to buy the product. Thus, when Michael,

STARS IN THE EYES

[Young people] have Stars in their eyes. With their eyes full of adoration, adolescents often believe their rock and roll heroes can do no wrong. They are always shocked to see their heroes fall. And they believe the myth that being a Rock Star fixes everything. . . . But being a rock star doesn't fix the anguish inside. It only exaggerates it. Fans are generally too naive to see this. The best the world of rock music can do is to "relate" to today's kids. Nirvana was not the top band because they were the best musicians around or because Kurt Cobain had the greatest voice. But they were able to identify with the anger and alienation of today's youth.

—Al Menconi
Media Update[5]

Cindy, Shaq, or Paula say something is good, young consumers think, *It must be good,* and they conclude that they must have it! Musicians, atheletes, and actors shine as the biggest stars in the teenage galaxy. When these men and women endorse sexual promiscuity, violence, or deviant lifestyles through their music and videos, kids think twice and often buy it.

The lifestyles of the performers. Celebrities like to say that they aren't role models, but they fill that role whether they like it or not. Kids idolize them and emulate the way they look, talk, and live. Marketers and publicists work hard to project a public image, a persona, for a star because they want to impress and influence the public. Unfortunately, the rich and famous teen idols often have well-publicized *depraved* lifestyles, filled with greed, drugs, sexual abuse, and even violence. Subtly, kids are influenced to live like their heroes. According to Al Menconi, an expert on popular music, "Fans claim that they don't listen to lyrics and that music doesn't affect them, which is never completely true. The party philosophy of these groups is communicated by far more than just lyrics. A band's costumes, stage shows, television/magazine interviews, and lifestyles combine to let a young fan know what his heroes believe and how to conduct his life."[6]

Constant repetition. A statement, even a lie or an absurd exaggeration, repeated enough times, will be accepted as truth. This is another underlying premise of effective advertising; thus, marketers expose potential customers to canned statements over and over again. Eventually, people will believe the statements, true or not, and spend their money. Kids listen to their favorite songs again and again on their stereos, at friends' homes, through headphones, and on the radio. The words of those songs become embedded in adolescents' minds. In addition, they see negative values lived out on the screen in movies. Eventually, teens begin to believe or at least tolerate the messages, even if the statements seem absurd at first or promote unlawful, extreme, or deviant activities.

Implicit permission. All children have strong urges and desires

VALUES NEUTRAL?

Those who defend contemporary rap music, with its extravagantly brutal and obscene lyrics, do not generally condone the conduct described in the songs; they suggest, rather, that it is inappropriate to judge such material on a moral basis. By the same token, producers of movies or TV shows that seem to glorify violent or promiscuous behavior do not assert that watching these entertainments is actually good for you. Instead, they maintain that the images they create amount to a "values-neutral" experience, with no real impact on the viewer and no underlying influence on society. The apologists for the entertainment industry seldom claim that Hollywood's messages are beneficial; they argue, rather, that those messages don't matter.

—Michael Medved
Hollywood vs. America[7]

that they would love to fulfill if given half a chance by their parents, teachers, or other authority figures. And let's face it, every person has a basic sinful nature (see Jeremiah 17:9 and Romans 3:23). Thus, the natural pull of human nature is downward, to do what is wrong. Now consider adolescents. In their changing bodies, minds, and emotions, sex becomes a powerful urge as hormones push toward sexual thoughts and activity. Without restraints, these urges will lead to sinful, selfish, and self-destructive acts. Teenagers need parents, teachers, coaches, pastors, heroes, and other responsible adults to model appropriate sexual behavior and to tell them to save sex for marriage.

At the very time when kids are so susceptible to lust and inappropriate sexual behavior, they are assaulted by the popular media. Instead of promoting restraint, abstinence, and mature patience, many of the songs, artists, and disc jockeys urge teens to play around, make love, and use others to gratify themselves. And this message is reiterated through movies and videos. It's as if adults are giving our kids permission to fulfill every lustful desire, no matter how wrong and sinful. Some adults may teach, "Just say no," but the society at large seems to scream, "Just say yes!"

Music, movies, and videos exert tremendous influence on our children, urging them to take a downward turn and go in the wrong direction in their lives.

The Conflict

It may seem obvious that parents should take action in this area, especially when the music and movies continually promote values that undermine our families' values and our Christian faith. Certainly we can't expect the government to step in and protect our children. And in this era of "free speech" and political correctness, the assault will only get worse. Therefore, par-

HOLLYWOOD VS. RELIGION

A half-century ago, motion picture makers were guided by a production code that assured viewers that Judeo-Christian values and people of faith would be portrayed in a positive light. But sadly, as Dr. Dobson explains, "For years now the entertainment industry has attacked our faith and undermined our value system. We must all get involved in the struggle to make Hollywood hospitable to religious values once again." When studios release films that mock our Judeo-Christian heritage and degrade religious faith, they must hear from us. Likewise, when a studio releases a praiseworthy film, we should write and express our appreciation.

—Focus on the Family flyer
included with the video *Hollywood vs. Religion*

ents are actually the *only* ones who can intervene and take action here. Yet, as we saw in the last chapter about television, instead of helping solve the problem, many parents actually contribute to it by ignoring the issue or even encouraging their children to become immersed in the popular culture.

Ignoring

Some parents really don't have a clue. They haven't listened closely or read the words to their kids' favorite songs, so they have no idea of the messages being communicated. They may even think that the music is not too bad, remembering that *their* music was also considered dirty by many in the older generation. Recently, on a major family radio station in Chicago, an on-air personality made that very point when asked whether a concert by a well-known group would be appropriate for a thirteen-year-old girl. He laughed and replied: "Sure. It's no worse than when we were that age—just different. We had our controversial groups too, you know." (He did warn the mother about the "moshing pit," however, explaining that, "it could get violent.")

Many of these moms and dads may not appreciate what their teenagers are listening to, but they don't want to seem to be out of touch or to be ogres, so they allow their sons and daughters to listen to whatever they want with friends or in their rooms. Similar thoughts occur when they consider television programs, videos, and movies. Instead of checking out the content of each show, they succumb to their teenagers' insistence that the show is fine, "Everyone watches it," and "So-and-so's parents allow it."

Although garbled words, loud instruments, or teenage slang obscure some of the messages in today's music, any adult who takes the time to listen will realize at once the drastic difference between the music of today and that of any previous decade. Thus I can only surmise that these parents haven't taken the time to find out what their kids are listening to. A friend shared recently that at his son's eleventh birthday party, three of the gifts were tapes of a music group that was hot among kids at school. After the party, when my friend told his son that he had never heard of the group, his son assured him that everyone at school was humming the group's latest song. As this interested father began to read the lyrics to the songs, printed on an insert, he became very concerned, noting that they were obscene and offensive. When he showed the lyrics to his son, the boy was genuinely surprised and explained that he didn't realize the group was like that. Together they decided to return the tapes to the store and exchange them for others that were acceptable. This dad took an interest, took time, and made a difference.

Parents who ignore the problem also trust the movie rating system and accept without question the recommendations of the movie reviewers, so they allow their kids to see many PG, PG-13, and even R-rated movies without a second thought. They may not appreciate the display of nudity or the four-letter words, but they have heard that the acting is "Oscar worthy," the director is a "creative genius," the costumes and scenery are "breathtaking," the cinematography is "inventive," or the story is "riveting." So with a cheery "Have a good time," they send the kids on their way, assuming the movie won't affect *their* kids. "After all," these parents say, "the kids aren't going to hear anything they haven't heard before." Or they may think that their kids will grow out of this phase, just as they grew out of *Sesame Street* and *Mr. Rogers' Neighborhood.*

Influencing

Many parents go beyond this point and actually influence their kids to embrace popular culture. They do so by allowing the kids to listen to any radio station, watch any television show, and buy whatever CD or tape they wish. At birthdays or Christmas, they give concert tickets, faddish clothes, posters of current teenage idols, and gift certificates for the music store.

Perhaps the greatest influence for teenagers making poor movie and video choices comes from the example set by the parents. Showing very little restraint in their own choices, these moms and dads go to all the latest shows, regardless of the ratings, and they bring negative, violent, or sexually explicit videos into their home. Certainly some movies, videos, books, and so forth are appropriate for adults and not for children; yet, parents will find it difficult to forbid a teenager to see a movie because it's "bad and wrong for them to see" when these parents see a parade of the forbidden movies themselves.

Parents also influence teens in this direction by allowing them to wear T-shirts promoting rock artists, driving them to the theater and allowing them to attend the movie of choice, and even renting questionable (though popular) videos for a birthday party or sleepover. A friend told me that some of his wife's work colleagues say that they urge their kids to "go for it." They think that it is foolish and even "psychologically damaging" to urge restraint.

So, What's a Parent to Do?

What are our choices as we see our teenagers envelop themselves in pop culture through music, movies, and videos? Do we, like my friend's wife's colleagues, tell them to "go for it," assuming they have the maturity and desire to listen with discernment? Do we "let them go," assuming they are going through a harmless stage of interest in rock music and music videos? Do we let them listen to and view whatever they want as long as the music and movies don't bother us? Do we forbid all rock music and movies?

Parents should be guarding their children against all assaults of body, mind, emotions, and spirit. Instead of having a hands-off attitude or seeing pop culture as harmless, we have other options—tough choices.

The Choice

Parents need to intervene, early and often, in making the tough choices about their teenagers' entertainment. While setting limits in the areas of music and entertainment may cause conflict between parents and teenagers, it can be done respectfully and effectively. Consider these suggestions.

Remember

Before jumping in with both feet, take time to reflect on *your* teenage years. Think about what pulled you toward your favorite bands, soloists, and actors. Perhaps you felt as if they spoke for your generation, or maybe following them was a symbol of your

NOT-SO-GRAND SLAM

Don't slam music. If you suggest that rock music is of the devil or if you put down this or that band, you will immediately trigger the defense mechanism built into every kid, and often just help push him or her toward all that forbidden fruit. Not all heavy metal or rap is bad just because some is. Remember, too, that kids are not as sophisticated as you may think they are. Many of them are exposed to double entendres and suggestive material but don't realize what is being said.

Also, keep in mind that most of these things (kinds of music, video games, etc.) are phases. They come and go, often intense at first, but after a while, slacking off or losing interest altogether.

—Rick Bundschuh
author and copastor at
Kauai Christian Fellowship, Kauai, Hawaii

rebellion and independence. More likely than not, however, your tastes followed your friends' tastes. That's also true with your kids. Their entertainment choices, especially their music, reflect the need to be accepted, to be liked, and to feel older. Teen music makes a social statement.

With this understanding, when you hear an offensive song, especially one that tops the charts, don't rail against "rock music" and "kids today" and give the impression that you are condemning your teenagers' friends and teenagers in general. This will turn off your teen faster than you can say "Top 40." Instead, turn the discussion toward *specific* choices without implying that all movies and music are bad. Then take the following positive steps.

Learn

Become a student of popular culture. Of course you won't be able to know everything about every band on the scene and every new release, but you can learn enough about the music, movies, and videos to make intelligent decisions and to guide your kids.

Begin by taking a quick trip to a music store. Flip through the top-selling CDs and tapes. Put on the headphones and listen to a few of the top tunes in the listening rooms. Most music stores carry lists of the Top 40 songs, and their clerks will be able to tell you about the most popular radio stations. Later, when driving by yourself, listen to those stations.

Subscribe to *Preview* and *Media Watch* or similar publications that provide helpful information on popular movies, videos, and music. The resources section at the end of this book gives additional help. To help spread out the cost, you may want to subscribe with other parents and then circulate each issue among the subscribers.

Be sure to check out the CDs and tapes that your teenagers are interested in or that they receive as presents. Usually the album covers will tell much about the direction of the music inside, but often each CD or tape has a printed copy of the words enclosed.

Also, talk with other parents to see what they know about specific music groups or movies. Find allies in this battle.

Model

Analyze your own entertainment choices. Although your choice of music doesn't include music filled with cursing and screaming, what kinds of values and lifestyles *do* your songs promote? I have heard many beautiful ballads that extol the virtue of premarital sex and adultery. Beware of thinking that soft music is *good* music. Easy listening or country songs can present values that are just as destructive as those endorsed in rock music.

And what kind of movies do you see? What values were portrayed and endorsed in those movies? Again, I have been surprised at the viewing habits of many Christian parents, who think nothing of going to an R-rated movie because they heard "it is good."

What videos do you watch in your home? In a recent small-group setting, adults talked about their favorite videos. Several of the adults, all Christians, talked about seeing R-rated videos. One of the couples giggled when they told how they had to pause the videos when their kids came in the room because "we certainly didn't want our kids seeing the steamy scenes." What did this experience say to this couple's children?

In Romans 14, Paul discusses the matter of being sensitive to younger and weaker believers. He states: "It is better not to eat meat or drink wine or to do anything else that will cause your brother to fall" (Romans 14:21). In a similar discussion with the Corinthians, Paul states, "'Everything is permissible'—but not everything is beneficial. 'Everything is permissible'—but not everything is constructive. Nobody should seek his own good, but the good of others" (1 Corinthians 10:23-24). An obvious application of these passages is that Christian adults should be sensitive to children and other weaker believers and should not do anything that would harm a person's faith or push that person in the wrong direction. Listening to questionable music or watching negative movies can do just that, and it isn't worth it. Discipline yourself and set a positive example for your children.

Teach

Help your kids to think critically. When you know of a problem with a song or movie, discuss it with them, focusing on the real issues. Emphasize the following biblical principles.

We learn a lot about people by how they speak. In teaching his disciples about inner purity, Jesus explained: "What comes out of a man is what makes him 'unclean.' For from within, out of men's hearts, come evil thoughts, sexual immorality, theft, murder, adultery, greed, malice, deceit, lewdness, envy, slander, arrogance and folly. All these evils come from inside and make a man 'unclean'" (Mark 7:20-23). Ask your teenagers these kinds of questions: What kinds of people would sing and say the lyrics in that song? What do you know about the lifestyles of your favorite performers?

Thoughts lead to actions. James 1:14-15 states, "Each one is tempted when, by his own evil desire, he is dragged away and enticed. Then, after desire has conceived, it gives birth to sin; and sin, when it is full-grown, gives birth to death." In other words, God is saying that if a person thinks about something long enough, he or she will do it, even if it's wrong. Ask your teenagers these kinds of questions: What messages do you hear in your music? What lifestyles, values, and morals are promoted in your favorite videos and movies?

Christians should focus on the positive. Paul exhorts all believers: "Whatever is true, whatever is noble, whatever is right, whatever is pure, whatever is lovely, whatever is admirable—if anything is excellent or praiseworthy—think about such things" (Philippians 4:8). Christians can fill their minds with all sorts of images, words, and ideas, but God wants us to focus on what is positive and uplifting. Ask your teenagers these kinds of questions: What positive, Christ-honoring values and lifestyles do your favorite songs, videos, and movies present? What can you do to fill your mind with good stuff?

Christians should guard against the wrong thoughts, ideas, and philosophies. Totally secular, anti-Christian worldviews fill contemporary music and movies. Paul's warning to the Colossians applies as well to us today: "See to it that no one takes you captive through hollow and deceptive philosophy, which depends on human tradition and the basic principles of this world rather than on Christ" (Colossians 2:8). Ask your teenagers these kinds of questions: What philosophy of life is presented in popular music and movies? In what ways is that different from the Christian worldview?

As you discuss these biblical principles, explain that you are not condemning all secular movies and music. Encourage your teenagers to be discerning in their entertainment choices. Teach them to analyze and to think critically.

SETTING THE STANDARD

What can a parent do to cushion the bumps
produced by the highway of media hype?

1. Set a family standard.
2. Spend plenty of time . . . personal time with each child.
3. Incorporate creative concepts into your family routine—concepts that will help your teens think critically about all forms of media.
4. Pray.
                                                        —Robert G. DeMoss Jr.
                                                        Learn to Discern[8]

Monitor

Even after explaining the biblical principles and discussing them together, you still should monitor your teenagers' listening habits, including radio stations. I'm not suggesting that you act like detectives and sneak through your teenagers' belongings, but you should be aware of what they are listening to. Don't assume that because you had one good talk with your teens about music and encouraged discernment that they will always do what is right. Remember, the pressure from friends and others continues. So keep in touch with what is going on.

Watch out for videos as well. Often the ratings are obscured or ignored in the video store. Also, many videos feature footage that was not in the regular movie. These "director's cuts" may be much worse than what the theaters showed. If you don't know anything about the video, assume the worst if a secular movie company has produced it.

One of the latest home invasions comes by way of the computer, with on-line services containing pornography and other questionable content. Computer-literate kids have easy access to this garbage and may happen to stumble upon it.

Prohibit

Don't be afraid to say no to certain performers and movies. For example, I don't think teenagers, especially Christians, should go to R-rated movies, no matter how critically acclaimed those movies may be. If *Hollywood filmmakers* think a movie rates an R, you can imagine how bad it must be. When producing movies, their thoughts center on money, not on parents and family values. So don't trust Hollywood to screen your movies for you.

Unfortunately, even most PG and PG-13 movies contain offensive words, scenes, and values. I find that these labels fool many Christian parents because "Parental Guidance" sounds so positive and "13" sounds so young. Remember, television shows carry no labels, yet many of the worst shows are broadcast during prime time, available for viewing by people of all ages. Most filmmakers' standards are so low that they act as if thirteen-year-olds are thirty and assume that these early adolescents can handle the barrage of nudity and four-letter words.

Parents who have the courage to prohibit certain movies and entertainers demonstrate to their kids that they care about them. Believe me, it is much easier for a young person to explain to a friend, "I can't go with you. My parents won't let me see R-rated movies" than to try to create and give a socially acceptable reason to decline the invitation.

Explain to your teenagers that your prohibitions also apply to videos shown at other kids' homes and at parties. This will be difficult to monitor, but you probably will be able to work with the hosts. Not realizing that certain videos may offend some kids and their parents, most parents will be open and responsive to what you have to say. It certainly won't hurt to explain your views. Gail and I have had parents thank us for calling, and they have changed videos because of our concerns.

When Gail and I chaperoned a high school choir trip, we traveled on highway buses that were equipped with video players and several small television sets mounted on the ceiling. We could show videos to the kids as we traveled, keeping them entertained and making the twenty-four-hour journey seem to go faster. As the head chaperone for my bus, I was able to choose from a wide selection of videotapes supplied by the students. My first two choices were easy—a Disney animation classic and a mystery thriller. The third tape I chose was rated PG-13 and was a comedy. I should have known better, but the plot looked innocent enough, and some of the kids were lobbying hard to see it. About a half hour into the movie, however, the story took a very suggestive turn, and so I stopped the tape. Over the loudspeaker, I explained that it wasn't an appropriate movie to watch. I expected howls of protests, but only a few voiced disapproval. Most knew I was right and appreciated what I had done. Later, the other chaperones thanked me. One even said, "That took guts." Most parents know that certain videos are inappropriate for kids to watch, but they may be intimidated by their children or confused because other parents seem to be open-minded and permissive. By expressing your views and gently taking a stand, you give them permission to do what they know in their heart is right.

DAD VETOES VIDEO

I remember one night when my friends came over with a video to watch at my house. As we were a third of the way into the video, my parents walked through the room and saw what was on. It wasn't R-rated or anything, but they were not happy. My dad said, "I'm not comfortable with you watching that video. Can we go get another one?" I was so embarrassed. I was sure my friends would never want to come to my house to watch a video again. I expected them to bad-mouth my dad and give me a hard time because of what he said. But they didn't. Two of them said nothing, and the third said, "That was a tough call for your dad to make. He's some guy." He respected my dad for what he had done. And you know what? My friends still like to come to our house.

—Dan, fourteen-year-old high school freshman

If you can't contact the hosting parent or you think that your call may cause a problem, tell your teenagers that they may leave the room if an offensive video is shown. Usually other activities are available in other parts of the house, or refreshments are available in the kitchen. The teen doesn't *have to* stay in the room and watch. By the way, let your teenagers know that if *any* party gets out of hand (because of no chaperones, drinking, abusive date, or whatever), they should call, and you will gladly pick them up or give them permission to drive home and leave the party early.

Guide

As we have seen in other areas, the operative principle with teenage entertainment is to *guide* rather than *block*. Look for alternatives to the obscene, violent, and pornographic choices. For example, most towns have more than one rock music station. Instead of banning all rock music, allow your son or daughter to listen to the station that doesn't play the raunchy music and on which the disc jockeys don't use obscene language. And don't prohibit a certain type of music; instead, ask your son or daughter to give you an honest appraisal of the content and lifestyles of specific bands and soloists. Then steer him or her to the positive performers.

Again, my experience with kids, in youthwork and with my own daughters, is that they know that certain music is unacceptable and actually appreciate it when someone turns it off or changes stations. Once, when Kara was fifteen, I was driving her and a group of friends home from high school. Kara sat in the front with me, and her friends were in the back. As is the case with most teenagers, the kids talked nonstop, and Kara continued to switch stations until she would find the right sound. I hadn't said much through all this, but as I heard the words to one song, I whispered to Kara (so her friends couldn't hear), "That's not a good song. Please change the station." Without arguing or missing a beat in the chatter, Kara quickly turned the

SPIRITUAL TEETER-TOTTER

The best means I have found for setting entertainment guidelines in the home is to use a spiritual teeter-totter. . . .

On a teeter-totter, the heavier the weight and the closer to the end you set the weight, the easier it will tip. Obviously, any philosophy on the selfish side of our spiritual teeter-totter will make it lean toward the Satanic end. The more blatant forms of selfish hedonism and immorality will increase the weight on the board. . . . A pound or two will not throw a spiritual life out of balance if it is already weighted down with biblical values and the meat of God's Word. But what about a life where there is little or no weight given to Jesus and the values he teaches? Then any weight given to the Satanic side, no matter how small, will tip the scales.

—Al Menconi
Media Update[9]

dial. Later we talked about the situation, and she agreed with me. Obviously I could have created an embarrassing scene if I had made some loud statement about the "junk on the radio" or had quickly turned it off. Guiding is much better than blocking.

Another direction in which to guide kids is toward contemporary Christian music. Today, Christian groups perform almost every style of music. Yet the songs are positive and uplifting, and many carry a powerful message. You can encourage your teenagers to move in this direction by

- helping find the Christian radio station that plays contemporary Christian music
- giving birthday and Christmas presents of CDs or tapes from top Christian artists
- paying for tickets to a concert by a quality Christian band or soloist
- checking out the music reviews in *Breakaway, Brio, Campus Life,* and *CCM* (See the resources section for subscription information.)
- playing contemporary Christian music CDs or tapes in the house

We are very fortunate to have so many great contemporary Christian artists. Only a couple of decades ago, there were few, if any, Christian rock bands, and the quality of their performances was questionable. Today, Christians present rap, country, hard rock, alternative, and many other musical styles, and the quality of the music, lyrics, and production rates with the top secular groups. Christian music provides a viable alternative to the Top 40 list.

Unfortunately, guiding and encouraging kids in the whole area of movies and videos is much more difficult. You will need to do much more research. *MOVIEGUIDE,* the *Alpha-Omega Film Report, Preview,* and the *McCullough Family Media Newsletter* can be a tremendous help, providing information and reviews. See the resources section for subscription information. When a good movie comes along, say yes! In fact, *jump* at the chance to let your teenagers see it. Most video stores have a very large selection of movies, so you are likely to find an acceptable movie there. Again, stick to your rules about the content of the movie, but say yes and pay for those that you know are good. And patronize video stores that restrict what kids can rent.

Pray

Nowhere do parents feel the assault on their values and the battle for their children more than in this arena of popular entertainment. So prayer is needed desperately. Pray that God will keep your kids safe from the attacks of the evil one. Pray for discernment and sensitivity as you deal with this very difficult area. Pray for courage to make the tough choices about which music, videos, and movies to forbid and which ones to permit. Pray for your teenagers' openness to God's work and your counsel in their lives. Prayer is the most important action you can take for your kids.

* * *

As kids enter adolescence, they pump up the volume and push the limits in other entertainment choices. This change can be shocking and disturbing to parents, especially those who are aware of the messages promoted through popular songs, videos, and movies and through the lifestyles of teen idols. What kids listen to and see can affect them profoundly, wearing away their defenses and even motivating them to sinful and self-destructive actions. Thus, responsible parents must make tough choices, taking action to protect their children and to move them in the right direction. The positive actions include remembering, learning, modeling, teaching, monitoring, prohibiting, guiding, and praying.

THINK IT THROUGH

1. When did your teenagers begin to listen to popular music? What are their favorite bands or soloists?
2. What movies did you later regret allowing your teenagers to see?
3. What arguments do your teenagers give for listening to music and going to movies that you don't approve of?
4. What will you do to educate yourself about current popular music?
5. How will you change your listening and viewing habits to model the kind of entertainment choices you want your teenagers to make?
6. When will you discuss with your adolescents the biblical principles that relate to entertainment?
7. What music, videos, and movies will you and your spouse prohibit your teens from listening to and watching (type, specific groups, etc.)?
8. To what alternative entertainment options will you guide your teenagers (radio stations, television shows, videos, and movies)?
9. What will you do to cultivate your teens' interest in contemporary Christian music?
10. When and where will you consistently pray for your teenagers?

CHAPTER **6**

"I'm Too Busy to Sleep"

*"Time is a precious commodity.
When you're late, you waste the
time of others around you."*
—Ozzie to David and Ricky
from "The Speech"

"WHERE'S JEFF?" Craig Sellars asks his wife, Marge, motioning toward the empty place at the dinner table. "He ought to be home by now!"

"Don't you remember?" Marge replies. "Tryouts for the solo-and-ensemble contest are tonight. Fortunately he was able to sign up for a late audition, so he's going to the choir room right after basketball practice. I told him to grab a sandwich at Mc-Donald's afterward because then he has to go to Chris's house to work on their history project."

"By the way, Mom," interrupts Sara, Jeff's nine-year-old sister, "I forgot to tell you, but Coach Lathrop called to remind Jeff of the soccer tournament this weekend in Blackbird Heights. The team will be meeting Saturday morning at six at the high school. Jeff needs to bring money for meals and the motel. They'll get back Sunday night at about eight."

"Oh. That's right! I had forgotten about that tournament," answers Marge. "Blackbird Heights is two hours away. There's no way we can get to those games. It's a good thing there's no basketball game Saturday night. Sometimes I wonder about club soccer, Craig. It's taking so much time. And final exams are coming up soon. When is Jeff going to study? For that matter, when is he going to sleep?"

"Now Marge, we've been through this before," her husband replies. "Jeff has real potential in soccer. It could lead to a scholarship! Jeff can take his books with him and study between games."

"Hey, wait a minute," interjects Jeff's little brother, Sam. "Saturday is 'Big Brother' night at the Y. Jeff promised to go with me!"

"He must have forgotten about the soccer tournament, Sam," Marge answers. "I'm sure he will go with you another time."

Sixteen-year-old Jeff is a high school sophomore who is a good student, a good musician, and an excellent athlete. In addition to studies, music, and sports, Jeff belongs to Star Raiders (a school antidrug club), French club, Student Council, and his church youth group. So far he has been able to fit it all in, with no noticeable effects on his grades, social life, church attendance, and family life. Recently, however, all of these areas and activities have been making increasing demands on Jeff's attention and time. Family and church have borne the brunt of his schedule adjustments. Also, Jeff has had less time to sleep, and he feels increased pressure on all sides.

The Challenge

In many ways, Jeff is a reflection of the times. Today's teenagers are expected to know more and do more than teenagers at any other time in history.

Technology

One reason for these expectations is the rapid advance of science and technology. Modern technology has revolutionized our lives. Think of it: Today we have personal satellite dishes, miniature video cameras, CD-ROM, notebook computers, cellular flip-phones, fax machines, the Internet, lasers, portable entertainment systems, and interactive videos. Our children are growing up with a technological sophistication that we only imagined or read about in science fiction novels.

Higher technology brings higher expectations because kids are expected to know more, sooner. In fact, at every level of society people seem to want everything instantly, adding to the pressures we all feel.

Two decades ago, futurists predicted that technology would

145

USE OF ELECTRONIC DEVICES BY TEENS

	National	Male	Female	13-15	15-17
Calculator	98%	99%	97%	98%	98%
Computer	97%	99%	95%	97%	97%
Answering machine	89%	91%	88%	88%	92%
Cellular phone	64%	64%	64%	64%	64%
Voice mail	24%	24%	24%	22%	27%
Pager/beeper	52%	55%	49%	48%	58%
Fax	31%	36%	25%	26%	38%
On-line service	30%	37%	24%	28%	35%
Teens who taught their parents on the above					
	59%	65%	52%	54%	66%

—"Teens and Technology: Together for Life"
YOUTHviews[1]

lead to vast amounts of leisure time, perhaps even a three- or four-day workweek. Instead, our ability to do things more quickly has heightened our expectations and increased our demands. Just ten years ago, I used a typewriter for all my "word processing." A computer allowed me to produce a better manuscript, and more quickly. But that didn't lead to more leisure time or a publishing schedule that gave me more space. Soon publishers expected everything "on disk," compatible with their computers. Ten years ago, we communicated by mail or phone. With the emergence of overnight-delivery services, fax machines, and E-mail, we are expected to send everything "now." Instead of adding an extra day to our weekends, modern technology has increased our work-loads, causing increased busyness and stress.

Technological advances have also given us many more choices and options in clothes, travel, appliances, and even food. In 1976 a typical supermarket offered nine thousand different products; sixteen years later, the same supermarket offered thirty thousand choices.[2]

These rapid advances in technology have led to a new generation gap. The jokes about kids having to program the VCR for
their parents are based in truth; actually, many adults are techno-
logically illiterate, which makes it increasingly difficult for parents
to help kids with their homework. Teachers, however, are employ-
ing technology more and more, using scores of computer appli-
cations in classrooms, the library, and even the "shop."

This pressure to do everything better and faster touches every
aspect of society, complicating and hurrying our lives.

Information

Perhaps the most significant result of modern technology is the
almost instantaneous communication of news and other world
events. A typical television newscast may feature live reports of
a devastating earthquake in Japan, destructive floods in Ger-
many, a terrorist bombing in Israel, a war in the former Soviet

GROWING UP TOO FAST

The media and merchandisers no longer abide by the unwritten rule
that teenagers are a privileged group who require special protection
and nurturing. They now see teenagers as fair game for all the arts of
persuasion and sexual innuendo once directed only at adult
audiences and consumers.

High schools, which were once the setting for a unique teenage culture and language, have become miniatures of the adult community.
Theft, violence, sex, and substance abuse are now as common in the
high schools as they are on the streets.

[One of the consequences of this premature adulthood and stress
is] more failure—because of excessive pressure to be successful, to ex-
cel academically, in sports, music, or extracurricular activities in order to "get into good schools"; kids themselves want desperately to
be popular and will do things they know are wrong.

—David Elkind
All Grown Up & No Place to Go[3]

Union, horrendous famine and genocide in Africa, rebels in Bolivia, the trial of O. J. Simpson in California, a mother who murdered her sons in South Carolina, and a kidnapping in Chicago. Then the news "magazine" programs analyze each significant incident, adding their own editorial comments. With dozens of cable channels and satellite links, information pours into our homes through television. Other information inlets include radio, newspapers, magazines, videos, quickly published books, and, through the information superhighway, computers.

This flood of information has led to the loss of innocence for our children. Aware of all that is going on in the world, they fear for their safety and carry the weight of the world. Think of it. When did you first learn about drugs? I didn't hear about drugs until high school, and then they seemed to be used only by poor and desperate people hundreds of miles away. Today, children in first grade know about drugs, drinking, child abuse, racism, war, poverty, and strikes, and they know the sordid details of the private lives of countless public figures.

Our children are hurried. As Dr. David Elkind, Professor of Child Study at Tufts University, has written, they are "all grown up with no place to go."

Competition

Americans have always been competitive; we want to be the best in every area. Our competitive urge has been heightened considerably, however, by the information age. Consider the proliferation of award shows. Years ago, we had Miss America and the Academy Awards. These days *TV Guide* lists the Emmys, Grammys, Golden Globe Awards, People's Choice Awards, American Comedy Awards, American Music Awards, Country Music Awards, Miss Universe, Miss Black America, and on and on.

Undoubtedly the greatest public competitive arena world-wide is sports. Professional athletes command astronomical salaries and the adulation of millions of fans. And each sport features a tournament to determine its "world champion." Every few years the world focuses on Olympic and World Cup champions; every year we discover the national champion in college football, basketball (Final Four), and baseball (College World Series), and in professional baseball (World Series), basketball (NBA Championship), football (Super Bowl), and other sports too numerous to mention.

Vaulted to superstardom through these events, the media blitz, and information technology, athletes exert tremendous influence on our kids, especially when these athletes gain access to the next level of influence—product endorsements. Even after trading tremendous success and adulation on the basketball court for mediocrity on the baseball field, Michael Jordan continued to be the highest paid American athlete. Young men and women still wanted to "be like Mike." Because of Michael Jordan, basketball shorts and "hang time" are longer, and little boys and girls try acrobatic shots and drive to the basket with their tongues out. Positive role models include Bonnie Blair, Kevin Johnson, David Robinson, Reggie White, Barry Sanders, Jackie Joyner-Kersee, A. C. Green, Michael Chang, Shannon Miller, and others. On the negative side, our kids want to argue like Charles Barkley, trash-talk like John Starks, cheat like Tonya Harding, taunt like Reggie Miller, throw tantrums like John McEnroe, provoke fights like Dennis Rodman and any number of hockey players, and show off and strut like Deion Sanders.

Combine technological advances, the age of information, and the American lust for being number one and we have cutthroat competition and professional attitudes pushing down to every level of athletics. These days, high school athletes dream of super-stardom and push for coveted scholarships. And the pressure on coaches to win is enormous; even in many junior high schools, "win, or lose your job" rules. I have watched park community football, swimming, and baseball programs. I've coached soccer, basketball, softball, and football. My own daughters have partici-pated in organized basketball, softball, soccer, volleyball, and swimming. So I have seen kids' sports up close, and I've felt the pressure. I also have heard parents berate umpires and referees and complain about the "incompetence" of coaches. And I have been surprised by my own feelings; in fact, at times I couldn't sleep the night after my soccer team lost. My wife would have to help me regain the proper perspective by reminding me that it was only a game—played by ten-year-old girls.

At times, coaches will nearly abuse their athletes in order to win an athletic contest. A few years ago in a high school where I worked in Campus Life, an all-star running back injured his

WHO WON?

In the spring of Bill's first year of junior high, he tried out for the school baseball team. Bill worked hard and never missed a practice. But winning was such an important consideration that the coach let Bill play in only *two* games—in the late innings and in the outfield where the opposing hitters were least likely to hit the ball. The coach didn't let him bat, not even once all year.

I often wonder if the coach, the players, the students, the fans— or anyone else who had anything to do with the team of thirteen- and fourteen-year-old boys—now remember what the won-lost record was that year. Somebody must remember, because it was so important to win then that one kid, who never missed a practice, could not bat once.

—Kevin Leenhouts
Campus Life Magazine[4]

knee in a football game. Although the injury wasn't serious, the doctor advised the boy to rest his knee for at least a week. The coach persuaded the young man to dress for the next game anyway, promising not to play him. After one offensive series, however, the coach sent in his star. A few plays later, a hard tackle buckled the weakened knee, and the boy had to be carried from the field. One coach's ego and obsession with winning led to a lost football season, a lost wrestling season (the boy was an all-state wrestler), and knee surgery for that young athlete.

No sport is immune. In our community, high school soccer and volleyball coaches expect their players to join club teams during the off-season. These private clubs not only cost hundreds and sometimes thousands of dollars, but they also involve many of hours of practice and travel each week. Even if the high school coaches were to say nothing about these clubs, the rising level of competition would almost require involvement. If parents want their teenagers to make the high school team, the teenagers should be in a club, or others will pass them up. And don't forget the sports camps and clinics in the summer. They also are big business.

In addition to academics and athletics, other activities such as music, theater, and speech also demand great amounts of commitment and time from participants. I was in college before I realized that I couldn't concentrate on academics, football, concert choir, and Youth for Christ at the same time; each interest and activity required a heavy investment of time and energy. At that point I had to choose. Today, however, the pressure to narrow one's focus occurs already in high school. Coaches seem to believe that the only thing that matters is their sport, so their players are expected to work nearly year-round on conditioning and skills.

This phenomenon also can be found in many junior high schools. Many young teens are being pressured to choose between sports and music or to choose a specific sport on which to concentrate. All of this contributes to the jammed schedule. Mix in other clubs, friends, and church activities, and we have a formula for chaos.

The Conflict

Every day has twenty-four hours. As much as we would like to have more, that's all the time anyone has. It's also true that a person cannot be in more than one place at a time. We shouldn't be surprised, therefore, when certain activities and interests get left behind in favor of others. We should expect battles for time and attention as the hurried pace of society spills over into family life. For example, when a father's job requires more travel at the same time that his high school son's music interests require extra practices, clinics, and performances, family time will suffer. In fact, some families may not be able to coordinate schedules to free a single week during the year for a vacation together. And when a daughter's club volleyball team plays in Sunday tournaments, her church involvement will suffer. She may have to leave the house at six o'clock in the morning, drive two hours to the tournament site, and return at eight or nine o'clock at night, thus eliminating Sunday school, worship, and youth group.

Clash of Values and Needs

Overly busy schedules lead to clashes of values. Teenagers and parents need to make choices, and these choices affect where we invest our time and our lives. If Christian parents were asked, "What's more important, family or job, schoolwork or extracurricular activities, church or sports?" probably most of them would answer, "family, schoolwork, and church." Yet, it is likely that the practices of these same families would demonstrate the opposite.

I have described how society has hurried our kids. Technology, information, and competition push them to grow up too fast and to fill every available moment with activity. But parents also contribute to this conflict. Subconsciously, many moms and dads try to meet their own needs through their kids. These parents can push in directions and toward activities that do not reflect their children's gifts, abilities, and interests.

Often this pressure stems from parents' unfulfilled desires and dreams. America has countless thousands of armchair quarterbacks (usually men), frustrated sports has-beens or wanna-bes who live vicariously through hometown sports heroes. Before their little boys can walk, these hopeful dads dress their babies in NFL properties and hang sports mobiles over the cribs. These men may even be heard saying things like: "He sure looks like a linebacker!" "Look at those hands—the next Ryne Sandberg."

SEEING THROUGH OUR EYES

When I was in first grade, I loved to sing. When it was my turn, I would stand up and sing clearly and happily, thoroughly enjoying myself. My teacher declared me singing champion.

Why did something as innocent and joyful as the music of small children have to be turned into a contest? The voices should have been a source of joy—not pride or shame, but my first-grade teacher thought that my talent should be brandished in front of my peers. My joy became a mixture of pride and shame, and as time went on, shame overshadowed pride. My teacher was the one who wanted a champion; all I wanted was to sing.

—Mary Wilke

153

"What's wrong with putting a basketball in there? Pete Maravich slept with one!" Many moms do this too, in other areas. It's fun to dream for our kids, imagining them achieving great success in sports, music, academics, or the theater. But we hurt them when our dominant, underlying motive is to fulfill *our* dreams, to bolster *our* self-esteem.

During the elementary school years, when children begin taking lessons and signing up for clinics and leagues, they may show desire and talent in a certain area. They may enjoy participating in a sport, playing an instrument, or joining a club just for the fun of it. During the junior high years, however, some narrowing occurs, as kids are "chosen" for school teams, musical groups, and plays. This process leaves behind many kids who didn't make the cut. Sometimes, particularly in sports, kids are chosen simply because they are big or tall. In fact, a boy who has grown sooner than his peers will tower over them and may be the school's football, basketball, and baseball hero. This boy, then, can build his self-concept around sports as he sees himself as an athletic stud, perhaps even bound for the NFL or NBA. Again, the parents enjoy the spotlight ("That's my son—the center, scoring all the points!"). Often, however, this young man begins to slip in his ranking as the other boys experience their growth spurts, and spurt right by him. By his junior year in high school, far from being the star, the former junior high jock may be riding the bench.

When parents sense this slip, in a sport or in any other high-profile activity, they may put even more pressure on their teenagers. Let's face it. Parents love basking in the reflected glory of their kids. As a result we may allow or even encourage them to compromise our family's values. And that's a problem.

SLOW DOWN

A central theme emerging in teenagers' reading and learning problems seems to trace back to the family. Parental attitudes are crucial. I'm liberal in many of my views, but I do think a solid family that isn't too busy to pay attention to their kids will produce students who do pretty well in school.

I think all of us need to slow down. These kids are expected to do too much, even the kids who come from fairly solid families. They're involved in sports and in so many other extracurricular activities that academics become unimportant. And some, of course, are driven to succeed by egocentric parents.

—Sylvia Skarstad
"View from the Chalkboard," *Youthworker*[5]

Stress

Jammed schedules also cause stress. You know it's true for you, right? Remember working twelve hours to meet an important deadline, then dealing with bills and conflict at home, and then rushing to a meeting . . . three or four days in a row? No doubt you soon became tired, irritable, and depressed. And countless cups of coffee during the day and aspirin at night gave only temporary relief. You were experiencing the effects of stress. You needed a break, a day off with no pressures, deadlines, or expectations. You needed to sleep in, relax, and recuperate.

In our fast-paced society, stress predominates, causing numerous physical problems including migraine headaches, ulcers, and heart disease. Stress can kill. According to Richard A. Swenson, M.D., disastrous consequences result from several contemporary stressors: change, mobility, expectations, work, control, fear, relationships, overload, illness and death, frustration and anger, time pressure, and competition. Describing "time pressure" Dr. Swenson writes: "The clock dominates our schedule as never before in history. We have more activities to arrive at and more deadlines to meet. Most of us are all too familiar with the feeling of panic as an appointed hour nears with work yet undone. We are ruled not by the week or day but by the minute." Explaining "competition" he writes: "Our modern world is an overly competitive place in which to live and work. When we couple a win-lose format with a pyramidal system, the winner gloats while the multitude of losers try to deal with the stress of not measuring up."[6] Dr. Swenson lists fifty psychological, physical, and behavioral stress disorders.

TIME
To understand how a society experiences time, examine its operative vocabulary. We talk of no time, lack of time, not enough time, or being out of time. Management in the workplace is so time-conscious that they practice time-management skills and time-compression techniques. They use a computerized time-piece to assure work efforts are time-intensive with no time lost. —Richard A. Swenson, M.D.
Margin[7]

If we adults struggle with the results of stress in our lives, imagine the potentially disastrous effects on our teenagers. Their stress can be compounded by peer pressure and their natural tendency to be disorganized. And they haven't learned adult mechanisms for dealing with pressure and stress. Our teens need time to be kids, to play, and to relax, instead of continually rushing from one activity to another and back.

So, What's a Parent to Do?

How do we help our teenagers make good choices about how they spend their time? How do we help them cut back when they need to? Do we take a hands-off approach, hoping they make it through without serious health problems? Do we enforce guidelines that restrict them to only one or two outside activities? Do we push them into every sport and activity *we* want them to explore? Do we allow them to invest time, energy, and our money in any sport or activity *they* wish to explore? How do we ensure that our teenagers get enough sleep and spend enough time on the essentials?

The Choice

Our choices in this conflict between schedule and values are tough because of the pressure in our own lives to do more and more, faster and faster. The choices are tough also because of the importance our society places on sports and on being number one. It won't be easy to say no to a coach or to our own egos. And it won't be easy to build margin into our lives.

Sabbath

One important choice is to honor the Sabbath principle. In the beginning, after God had finished creating the heavens and the earth, "on the seventh day he rested from all his work. And God blessed the seventh day and made it holy, because on it he rested from all the work of creating that he had done" (Genesis 2:2-3). We don't know why God took a "day" to rest (certainly he wasn't stressed out or tired), but this act, at the beginning of time, became the model for his human creations to follow. Listen to the fourth commandment and its rationale: "Remember the Sabbath day by keeping it holy. Six days you shall labor and do all your work, but the seventh day is a Sabbath to the Lord your God. On it you shall not do any work, neither you, nor your son or daughter, nor your manservant or maidservant, nor your animals, nor the alien within your gates. For in six days the Lord made the heavens and the earth, the sea, and all that is in them, but he rested on the seventh day. Therefore the Lord blessed the Sabbath day and made it holy" (Exodus 20:8-11). God knows that every week human beings need one day that is totally set aside for personal renewal, for worship and rest.

Jesus knew this truth and practiced it during his life on earth. Mark explains that so many people were coming to Jesus and the disciples that they hadn't taken time to eat. So Jesus said, "Come with me by yourselves to a quiet place and get some rest" (Mark 6:31). Often, Jesus would retreat from the crowds to spend time in prayer and rest.

God tells us to rest, and Jesus provides a good example; yet we busily rush from one activity and responsibility to another, trying to ignore this need. And we suffer the consequences.

Choosing to build Sabbath rest, *margin*, into your family's life

THE RHYTHM OF FAMILY TRADITIONS

Growing up in a Jewish household, I was familiar with traditions such as lighting the Sabbath candles on Friday night, lighting the Hanukkah lights for eight evenings, and celebrating the Passover. Christianity doesn't have as many traditions, so neither do Christian families.

Christian parents should establish traditions that draw them closer to each other and to the Lord. For example, they could eat together four nights a week, with the phone off the hook; the parents could make bedtime a special time of conversation, prayer, and bonding; the family could prepare for Sunday on Saturday night; kids could plan special family activities, such as going to a sporting event, a movie, or a concert; the father could schedule appointments with each child for breakfast at McDonald's.

Get into the rhythm of family traditions.

—David Olshine
Director of Youth Ministries, Columbia International University

will not be easy. It may mean reorganizing your personal schedule. Certainly it means setting aside the Lord's Day for worship and personal renewal. In addition to church, look for ways to relax and have fun together as a family. Don't allow work, business travel, or volunteer responsibilities to steal time from this important day. Build family traditions and make vacation days and weeks a priority.

Also carve out margin time each day for personal renewal. Recently I have been convicted about this. My usual evening routine includes watching the ten o'clock news and then about the first half of *The Late Show with David Letterman*, getting to bed at about eleven o'clock. In the morning, I read the paper while I eat breakfast, and then I go to work. I decided that by eliminating the news, Letterman, and the newspaper, I could go to bed earlier. Then I could get up earlier to spend time in prayer and to be with my high school daughter, Dana, as she eats breakfast and leaves for school. Certainly nothing is inherently wrong or sinful about *Eyewitness News*, *The Late Show*, or the *Chicago Tribune*, but I have been spending too much time with them and not with the Lord or with my wife and daughter. This change in routine causes no hardship to me or my family.

Also, to build margin in my life I am planning to reduce my outside commitments. Currently I have ten volunteer responsibilities in church and in the community. At times, these responsibilities bump into each other, filling a week or two with chaos. So I am evaluating them to see which ones line up with my stated values and priorities.

In the family, Sabbath rest begins with the parents—with you. Be a good example of the fourth commandment. Then you will be able to help your children build margin into their lives.

MARGIN

God never intended for time to oppress us, dictating our every move. That was progress's idea. Instead, time was simply his way of making sure everything didn't happen all at once. We are free to use it, and if we are wise, we will use it with eternity in view.

Regaining margin in our use of time is one way of restoring freedom to overloaded lives. With time margin we can better enjoy what we are doing, we have a more wholesome anticipation of our next activity, we are more contemplative, we are more in touch with God and with each other, we have more time for service, and we actually delight in *looking for the divine interruptions he sends us.*

—Richard A. Swenson, M.D.
Margin[8]

Discussions later in this chapter will prepare you to help your kids schedule their time and say no to that extra activity or Saturday sleepover.

Schedule

Packed schedules can cause conflicts with our personal and family values. I remember when Los Angeles Dodger pitcher Sandy Koufax refused to pitch in a World Series game because it fell on a Jewish holiday. A few years ago, an outstanding guard on a junior high girls' basketball team I was coaching refused to play on Sunday—she was a Mormon. The Hall of Fame athlete and the thirteen-year-old girl had the courage of their convictions; in contrast, many *Christians* seem very willing to set aside worship, family, and other important interests and events for other activities and responsibilities. When Jesus commands us to "seek first his kingdom and his righteousness" we glibly present our lineup of values, with God and family heading the list (Matthew 6:33). But then we don't live what we profess.

Aligning the schedule with your values will involve tough choices, for you and your teenagers.

Perspective
When children are young, they need to explore a variety of interests, and most communities provide learning and performing opportunities through the community or private organizations. Countless classes and clubs allow kids to explore and try the whole range, from lessons in music, swimming, dancing, ice

CAFETERIA FOOD FOR THOUGHT
If you believe that your family should have at least one meal together each day and your teen is too busy before school for breakfast or at night for dinner, here is the solution: Tell your teenager that you will be glad to come to school and have lunch with him or her in the cafeteria. *He or she will be home for dinner!*

—Bill Sanders
youth speaker, author, and television host of *Straight Talk*

skating, tennis, and gymnastics to clinics in cheerleading, soccer, football, and basketball; from teams and leagues to children's choirs and theaters; from neighborhood groups to church youth groups. Parents may become frustrated as they buy the soccer shoes and shirt or pay for the guitar lessons, only to have their children turn their attention elsewhere, requiring new equipment or clothes. But this experimentation can help parents learn more about their kids. Let's face it, sometimes kids want to play a sport or learn an instrument simply because they saw it on television or because their friends are involved.

When kids reach junior high age, their schools offer an additional menu of activities: band, choir, drama, intramural and varsity sports, and a number of clubs. Early adolescents want to achieve, to be good at something, so they join, sign up, and try out. Again, this process is positive because it helps young people learn about themselves. On the negative side, however, too many parents, teachers, and coaches begin exerting pressure, expecting more from their star performers.

If you find it difficult to be objective about your teenagers' abilities, gifts, values, and future, you need a fresh perspective, a new look from a different angle. Call a time-out. Back off a bit, and take a realistic look at your teenagers.

First, look at the past. Think back to those elementary school and junior high days of lessons, clinics, and Little League. Look for threads of positive experience and performance, answering these questions:

- In what activities did my teenagers have the most fun?
- In what activities did they perform well?
- In what activities did they seem the most interested?
- Which activities helped develop their God-given talents and abilities?

Next, take a close look at your teenagers' present activities. Be sure to include activities related to school, neighborhood, and church. Analyze them by answering these questions:

- Which activities do my teenagers enjoy the most?
- Which activities help them to develop physically, socially, mentally, or spiritually?
- Which activities build their self-esteem?

- For which activities do my teenagers exhibit the most potential?
- Which activities cause little or no stress?
- Which activities cause no conflict with the family's values?

Then look ahead. Most teenagers will not have the maturity to make decisions with the future in mind. As you seek to help them, answer these questions:

- Which present activities will help them in college, career, marriage, etc.?
- In which activities are my teenagers likely to be involved ten years from now?
- What new activities will help my teenagers prepare for the future?

After taking this careful look at your teenagers, place all of their current activities and potential new ones into the following categories (you may list an activity in more than one category):

- These activities definitely enhance my teenagers' self-esteem and are helping build them physically, socially, mentally, or spiritually.
- These activities cause little stress and do not conflict with our family's values.
- Our teenagers have exhibited great potential for success in these activities, which will help them in the future.

Talk over your analysis with your teenagers. Use these questions to help you make the tough choice of which activities to emphasize, which ones to de-emphasize, and which ones to drop.

MAKING IT

In a book, a former Miami Dolphins lineman says: "I guarantee you Christ would be the toughest guy who ever played this game. . . . If he were alive today, I would picture a 6' 6", 260-pound defensive tackle who would always make the big plays and would be hard to keep out of the backfield. Yes, he'd make it with the Miami Dolphins today, and he would be a star in this league."

In a much smaller book, a man named Isaiah (in a very different league) wrote: "See my Servant shall prosper; he shall be highly exalted. Yet many shall be amazed when they see him. . . . In God's eyes he was like a tender green shoot, sprouting from a root in dry and sterile ground. But in our eyes there was no attractiveness at all, nothing to make us want him. We despised and rejected him—a man of sorrows, acquainted with bitterest grief."

I don't know if I'm a positive thinker. But if Christ were an overgrown Miami Dolphins defensive tackle instead of the Morning Star, I don't think I'd have a change in life.

I have no doubt he could play in the National Football League. I have no doubt he could be the world's toughest jet fighter. I have no doubt he could be the greatest tap dancer the world has ever seen. More significantly, I have no doubt he could turn stones into bread.

But it seems a bit beside the point.

—Kay Linskoog
The Other Side[9]

Fifteen-year-old Susan, for example, is a member of the high school choir, marching band, and flag team. She enjoys acting and would love to have a part in the spring musical. She also plays softball and is active in her church youth group. The school groups do not perform or play on Sunday, so she has no conflict with church. But her Monday-through-Saturday schedule has become overloaded, causing her grades to suffer. Susan loves music and plans to study music in college, so her parents encourage her to continue with the school choir and band but to choose among the flag team or softball or the musical for her other extracurricular involvement. Susan decides to drop the flag team. Then, because she wants to do both spring softball and the spring musical, her parents encourage her to skip the high school softball season and play in a summer league instead.

Brian, a high school sophomore, is an outstanding athlete, a member of the varsity soccer, basketball, and baseball squads. The coach of each sport has been pressuring him to concentrate only on that coach's particular sport and to play it year-round, both in school and in off-season clubs, making it impossible for Brian to participate in any other sport. The coaches continually remind Brian of scholarship possibilities if he gains success in that particular sport. Brian likes all the sports and all the head coaches, so he doesn't know how to respond. In talking over the situation with his parents, however, Brian realizes that his goal to become a doctor means that schoolwork comes before sports. His parents point out that the off-season club teams usually play on Sundays and during the traditional family vacation times. They also explain that although an athletic scholarship would be nice, attending the *right* university is more important than a *free* one. Brian decides to continue playing all three sports in school for now and not to join any off-season club teams.

Janelle has all accelerated classes, so homework and special projects take much of her time. In addition, she belongs to the debate team, Math Club, the National Honor Society, the Faculty-Student Advisory Council, and the Academic Bowl squad. Janelle enjoys Campus Life club when it doesn't conflict with homework or another meeting, and she regularly tutors under-privileged kids on Saturday mornings. Heading into her senior year, however, she feels overwhelmed and would like to develop her social life. Janelle's parents talk with her and help her analyze her options and priorities. As a result of their conversations,

Janelle decides to discontinue her involvement in Math Club and the Faculty-Student Advisory Council and to get more involved in Campus Life and in the church youth group.

Some parents and teenagers may conclude that involvement in intramural sports makes more sense than dealing with the pressure of competitive school sports. Some may decide to drop certain activities and add others that have more positive implications for the future. For example, I invested much of my high school years playing football and basketball. Yet as an adult, I spend most of my time writing and speaking. It seems that working on the high school speech team or the school newspaper would have been much more helpful for me in the long run.

* * *

Resist the rat race and refuse the temptation to meet your needs through your kids. Build margin into your life and focus on what is truly important. Analyze the past and present with a view to the future. Discuss all the options with your teenagers. Then together make the tough choice of focusing on certain activities and de-emphasizing or dropping others. Help your teenagers understand margin and the conflict of values. Then help your teenagers choose God's best.

THINK IT THROUGH

1. In what ways has technology rushed and pressured your family?
2. How has the information explosion affected your family?
3. In what ways has your competitive nature affected your family's schedule?
4. What evidence of stress do you see in yourself and in your family?
5. When are you tempted to meet your own needs through your kids?
6. What family values do you want to protect?
7. In what way does your schedule conflict with those values?
8. In what ways do your teenagers' schedules conflict with those values?
9. What can you do to help build Sabbath rest, *margin,* into your teens' life?
10. When will you analyze your teenagers' activities and schedules?
11. When will you talk with your kids about schedules and priorities?
12. What tough choices will you make in this area?
13. What will make those choices difficult?
14. How will you help your teenagers make decisions resulting in God's best for them?

CHAPTER 7

"School . . . Who Needs It?"

"It's funny how some people turn out to be fair-weather friends."
—Ozzie to David and Ricky
from "That Goshdarn
Thornberry"

BAM! THE BACKDOORSLAMS. Hurried footsteps sound through the kitchen, down the hall, and up the front stairs. Looking up from her magazine, Edith Rose calls after her teenage son. "Matt!" No answer. She calls louder, "Matt! Come here. I need to talk with you."

"Just a second, Mom," comes the muffled reply, as Matt yells back through the sweatshirt he is pulling over his head. A few minutes later, he skips down the stairs and into the family room.

"It's late. Where have you been?" questions Matt's mother. "And now where do you think you're going? We'll be eating in about half an hour."

"Some of us went over to Doug's house for a while after school," Matt answers calmly.

"What did you do there? Were Doug's parents home? Who was with you?" interrupts his mom.

"Oh, Mom, it was no big deal," Matt replies, shoving his hands into his jeans and shrugging his shoulders. "We just walked to his house, shot a few hoops, talked, hung out—you know."

"Well, all right. But I'm not sure I like you spending all that time with Doug and his friends," answers Matt's mother. "Anyway, what about homework? Don't you have a history test coming up soon? Your grades last quarter weren't very good, as you recall."

"I don't have any homework. I did it at school. Besides, Doug already took that history test and said it was easy," explains Matt. "Well, I've gotta go. Mike's picking me up. There he is now. We're going to the mall. I'll grab something to eat there!" Matt turns and walks quickly toward the door.

"If you're sure you have your homework done. I don't know if I like you being gone all the time. Be careful and get home before ten!" she calls after him.

Bam! The front door slams. Mrs. Rose shakes her head and mumbles to herself, "That kid and his friends!"

Edith Rose is a concerned mother. The older of two children, Matt has always been an above-average student and a good example to his little brother, Peter. Recently, however, in this sophomore year of high school, Matt has become less and less interested in school. Instead, he spends blocks of time with friends, and when he is home, he just sits in his room with the door closed and listens to music. His grades have begun to slip, and he is involved in no extracurricular activities.

Business that requires her husband to travel during the week leaves Edith feeling the heavy pressure of parenting a teenager. When she expresses her concerns to her husband, Jared, he assures her that Matt is normal and is just going through a phase. "He'll snap out of it," Jared usually replies.

Edith isn't so sure. Matt's not doing anything wrong or getting into trouble, but he's not doing anything with his life either. That's what is confusing. Matt seems to be wasting so much time!

The Challenge

Edith and Jared Rose's challenge is different from the challenge described in the last chapter. While Marge and Craig Sellars' son Jeff was overly busy with school and related activities, Matt Rose just doesn't seem to care about school. His parents wonder if he's spending too much time with friends. They fear that he is "wasting" time that could be better spent on schoolwork. Matt feels that *school* may be the waste of time.

Wasted Time

In some ways the debate about wasted time is a matter of perspective. Many parents are compulsive about using time well.

These parents can push their kids to be productive, often communicating that they consider any relaxation or socialization to be a total waste. Yet everyone needs time to recoup and regroup.

At the other extreme stand (*sit* or *recline* would be better descriptions) teenagers. For many kids, wasting time is a normal activity, and *work,* homework or any other kind, is a four-letter word. That shouldn't surprise us. Most American kids live very sheltered lives. That is, their needs are met by others. While that is particularly true for infants and young children, many adolescents believe that the world still revolves around them. Even after decades of youthwork, I am still amazed at how self-centered and self-absorbed teenagers can be. I realize that in our society, many children, especially those in poor or abusive environments, are forced to face major crises and adultlike responsibilities. But most children, especially those from positive and loving homes, have a rather limited perspective on life and work. That's not bad; it's just a fact we have to deal with.

One reason teenagers seem to waste time is *inertia*. Inertia is the tendency of a resting object to remain at rest or of a moving object to continue in the same direction unless it is affected by an outside force. Although young people aren't "objects," they tend to stay "at rest." And if they are going in a certain direction, they will tend to continue in that direction. The challenge for parents, teachers, coaches, and youth leaders—all of whom have higher goals for these kids than the kids do for themselves—is to be the "outside force" that will get them moving or will change their direction.

Perhaps the biggest consumer of adolescent time is hanging out with friends. To some teenagers, friends mean everything. This intense interest in friends begins in early adolescence. Parents notice the change when the phone seems to grow out of the teen's ear. These kids can talk for hours about everything . . . or nothing. And with the growing interest in the opposite sex during the junior high years, the interpersonal intrigues are almost endless. Immersed in learning social skills, early adolescents become consumed with relationships. Groups of friends assume great importance as well, especially as early adolescents look to groups of peers to provide acceptance and security against the cruelty that life in middle school can bring.

Teenagers enjoy "hanging out," just spending time together with no particular agenda. They may sit in a friend's room and talk while listening to CDs. They may take a long walk around the neighborhood or a drive around town. Or they may go to a neighbor's driveway or the park and shoot baskets. On the positive side, this time spent with friends can be characterized as "socialization" and "relaxation." Certainly nothing is inherently wrong with spending time with friends. On the negative side, many people would say that this unsupervised hanging out can lead to trouble, including drinking, smoking, vandalism, and other mischief. ("Idle hands are the devil's workshop.") Either way, it's not a very productive use of time, especially as a daily routine.

A third activity that consumes a great deal of adolescents' time is watching television. Discussions in chapter 4 sufficiently prove that time in front of the television is often wasted time.

School Life Suffers
The major casualty of this lifestyle is school involvement. Because most kids have little natural motivation for studies and education, they will tend to let their schoolwork slide. With friends and television consuming most of their free time, they try to coast through their classes. School just isn't that important to them, and this value may be reinforced by their friends.

Parents often wonder which comes first. Do teenagers lose interest in school and *then* find friends who feel the same way and who reinforce their way of thinking? Or do teenagers' friends influence them to devalue education? Actually, it can happen either way, or both ways at the same time. Kids are influenced heavily by their peers; there's no doubt about that. But usually they have to buy into what those peers are saying or pressuring. In seventh grade, Kenny begins to struggle in his classes, and his grades begin to slip. He shows little concern and even seems to take pride in the fact that he is having problems in some classes, bragging to his friends about his D or F on a test or assignment. They laugh with him and talk about the "stupid" teacher. Unless Kenny collides with an outside force that will change his academic direction, he will continue to gravitate to peers who have the same values. Kenny eventually will make academic underachievement his style.

Usually the slide to indifference about school begins in junior high as early adolescents experience great change in all areas of life. In chapter 3 we discussed how these changes affect their relationship to church and spiritual matters. Schoolwork and grades also suffer.

The mental transformation during these years can be as dramatic as the physical and social changes. Most early adolescents still think in concrete terms; that is, they find it difficult to understand concepts. They take statements literally and focus on what is happening right now. By the time they reach late junior high or high school, teenagers should be able to track with adults who talk about concepts and ideas. Junior high *teachers*, however, are adults who can think conceptually, and much of their curricula deal with concepts. Therefore, even though these teachers have taken courses in child development and know that many of their students may still be in the "concrete operations" stage, they will gravitate toward students who have made the transition into conceptual thinking. In Kenny's history class, Mrs. Anderson is always talking about cycles and trends. The only "cycle" Kenny understands is his "bi-cycle." Melissa, however, knows exactly what the teacher is talking about; she grasps the concept. As a result, Melissa not only gets better grades than Kenny does, but she also receives affirmation and approval from Mrs. Anderson. Kenny begins to hate history class.

Social changes and pressures also affect early adolescents' attitudes toward school and grades. In some circles of friends, it isn't "cool" to get good grades. A few years ago, I sat in the back of a middle school awards assembly. I was impressed with the faculty's attempt to give each student an award so that no one would feel left out. Even the least motivated, most disruptive, and seemingly incorrigible student received recognition: "Most Potential" or "Most Improvement Last Week" or something similar. Every time a faculty member would announce an award, the recipient would be applauded by the crowd and cheered by his or her friends. Students were honored for achievement in sports, music, art, citizenship, drama, school spirit, and so forth. But when the teachers began to announce the academic awards, the atmosphere changed, especially when kids were singled out for getting straight A's. When a girl's name was announced, she was greeted with applause as she stepped forward to accept the certificate and handshake from the teacher. It was different with the boys. Each time a boy was honored for making the honor roll, his friends laughed and gave him a hard time as he walked forward. Most of the guys seemed genuinely embarrassed about getting good grades. Their male peers did not value academic achievement.

Although I have used boys to illustrate this problem, it is not their exclusive domain. Girls who don't yet think conceptually and whose friends are struggling with their grades will also find it easy to devalue school and education. They will get into the habit of sliding by and making excuses to their parents for their grades: "The teacher is unfair," or "No one understands this class," or "No one in the class got above a C on the test," or "How can I use this stuff anyway?" They may even begin to cheat rather than do the work. In some peer groups, getting away with cheating is highly valued.

Unless this drift away from school, studies, education, and activities is stopped, it can lead to serious problems.

The Conflict

Conflict arises because teenagers tend to be shortsighted. They live for the present and often do not see the value of the hard work required to gain a solid education. As adults, we know that during the junior high and high school years, young people pour the foundation on which they will build their future. Our job is to help them see the long-term importance of staying in school and getting an education.

Learning

First, school is a valuable experience because of what students learn: reading, literature, math, science, arts, foreign language, vocational skills. Teenagers often excuse their indifference to certain classes by saying, "Why do I need to study math? I'll never use this." The truth, however, is that whatever the eventual vocational choice, successful adults need to know how to function with numbers, how to communicate, how to understand the world and the people around them, and how to read. Tragically, many adults today are functionally illiterate. Passed from grade to grade, they were allowed to graduate without having learned how to read. But people can fake it for only so long. In the end, the truth will come out. It is vital for young people to stay in school and to *learn,* to master each stage of the basic intellectual skills.

In addition to learning facts, figures, and skills in school, students gain a worldview. In a geography class, for example, students learn about the new nations that have risen from the former Soviet Union. A typical teenage response to that course of study may be, "This is stupid. I'll never travel there!" But geography concerns more than a future travel itinerary; in that class, students get the big picture: they learn about the world. The same could be said for social studies, science, music— almost any subject.

A teenage friend once asked me, "Why do I have to take this? What's the point? What good is it going to do me?"

I answered, "If nothing else, you'll be able to carry on an intelligent, adult conversation."

Studying a wide variety of subjects opens students' minds and eyes. A liberal education broadens their perspective and provides tools for *life,* not just for making a living.

Opportunity
Another important reason for taking education seriously involves young people's identity. The most pressing psychological-emotional task for middle adolescents is discovering who they are and where they fit in the world. Are they athletic? musical? outgoing or shy? intelligent? skilled? Will they be good executives? salespeople? spouses? citizens? technicians? leaders? Answers to these questions appear when kids begin to discover

their talents, capabilities, and aptitudes. This happens in classes, through relationships, in personal study, and through specific experiences.

Most people have hidden abilities—strengths and potential greatness waiting to be discovered. A high school friend and I stood with the crowd to sing the national anthem at a basketball game. I was surprised to hear his clear tenor voice ring out, hitting "the land of the free" with ease. Seconds later I commented on his good voice and asked if he was in the school choir. Surprised at my reaction, he answered no and explained that he had never seen himself as "musical." Who knows, perhaps my friend could have been the next Luciano Pavarotti or Steve Green or Larnelle Harris if his parents and teachers had encouraged him to develop this talent. But he didn't even know he could sing.

How did you get into your line of work? Most likely, you became interested in that career in a class and through affirmation by friends and significant people in your life. What's your favorite avocation? How and when did you get into it? Probably you heard or read about it, decided to try it, and enjoyed it.

Our junior and senior high schools provide a multitude of classes and experiences that help kids learn about themselves, uncovering all sorts of hidden abilities and introducing them to new ventures.

Education is not confined to the classrooms. Extracurricular activities provide a wealth of experiences. Schools offer a whole range of clubs, sports, organizations, performances, and other creative outlets: student council, class leadership, publications, music, drama, speech, interscholastic and intramural athletics, academic teams, subject-related clubs, service clubs, committees, and many others. Each activity helps teens learn more about themselves and develop skills. In the process they also have fun!

Young people who drop out of school or who just show up and do the minimum cheat themselves out of the excitement of learning and miss great opportunities.

Friendship

A third benefit of a well-rounded school experience is the social development it offers. Adolescence is a time of intense social exploration and development. During the teen years kids learn how to get along with others, how to carry on a conversation, how to respect people who are different, and how to understand and relate to members of the opposite sex. Schools, through their classes and their activities, provide many opportunities for learning those social skills: class discussions, group projects, speeches, teamwork, extracurricular activities, competitions, performances, elections, and parties. Even negative relational experiences like friendship conflicts, peer pressure, and rejection can provide opportunities for learning and growing.

Impact

The last time a cross section of the community comes together under one roof is in high school. Afterward, kids scatter among various interests, pursuits, and locations: some go into the military; others continue their education at a distant university or college; some get married; some work full time; others attend community colleges or technical schools. The high school years, therefore, present the ideal time to make a significant impact for Christ on the community. In addition, numerous studies have shown that it becomes increasingly difficult to reach people for

Christ as they get older. Thus, the junior high and high school years are crucial for evangelism.

Christian young people need to be awakened to their great God-given privilege and responsibility to reach their friends for Christ. Youth leaders need to motivate and train them to make a difference on their campuses, to love others, to stand for the truth, and to share the gospel. Christian kids should become involved in every area of campus life. Those who merely put up with high school and limit their involvement to going to classes miss out on seeing God work through them to change lives.

School provides many opportunities for learning content, broadening perspective, discovering identity, deepening friend-ships, and making an impact. These years build for the future, and they pass very quickly. Many adults look back with regret, wishing that they had been more involved and had done more. They wish they had run for office, auditioned for the play or musical, joined the newspaper staff, competed in a sport, taken art classes, studied seriously, or tried out for debate. Kids are kids only once. When these school years are gone, they are gone forever.

So, What's a Parent to Do?

I am amazed at how easily some parents give up and allow their adolescents to do as they please. This is especially true during the high school years. When children are in junior high, parents still pressure them to do homework and try to persuade them to become involved in school activities. But, tiring of the battles and the whining, many parents withdraw from the battle or resign themselves to the fact that their kids just aren't cut out for school. These parents allow their teenagers to spend most of their time away from academics and the campus. How can we resist that temptation?

The Choice

Parents will have to make tough choices regarding school, studies, homework, and extracurricular activities. These choices will be difficult, not because they require great wisdom and discernment—most parents understand the importance of education—but because they will take energy and perseverance. Remember, to overcome inertia, an object must be acted on by an *outside force*. That's you. Overcoming the influence of peers also will require great effort.

Priority

Turning the tide for education begins by making schoolwork a high priority in your home. Obviously, this perspective needs to be communicated long before a student reaches junior high, but it's never too late to start.

Before a new school year begins, discuss with your spouse what expectations you will have of your teenagers. Then hold a family meeting in which you outline your standards for homework and grades. Speak calmly and firmly, explaining the importance of scholastic achievement. Announce that homework comes first, before television, friends, phone calls, and play. Describe the penalties for poor performance and the rewards for following the rules and doing well. Let your teenagers know that you want to trust them and that you expect the best of them. Designate special study areas and times, emphasizing that *no one,* not even parents, should bother or interrupt a person who is studying.

After the meeting, get together with each teen individually to discuss specific grades and study habits. Bring out a recent report card and talk through the successes and setbacks of the previous year. Then work through the new school schedule and talk about each class.

Next, discuss the study area. Most kids want to read in poor light, while lying down, and with the music on. Insist on a quiet, well-lit place that is free from distractions, even if that means moving furniture to provide space for your teens to study. If your teenagers' grades have been slipping, explain that you expect to be told about *all* homework assignments, quizzes, reports, and exams. And emphasize that your teens should bring home all graded and returned tests and papers.

COVENANT

Make a covenant with your teens. In it, be clear about your expectations. They can spend time with their friends *if* they are first responsible about their schoolwork. In return, explain what you will do to help them entertain their friends. *If* they maintain a certain grade point average, you will provide snacks so that your teenagers' friends will feel free to hang out and eat (a surefire winner with teens!) at your place.

—Kara Eckmann
Director of College Ministry, Lake Avenue Church, Pasadena

This will take effort and perseverance. Insist on compliance, and stick with the plan. You may have to forgo watching the NFL or your favorite television program in order to quiz your seventh grader about science. You may even have to study the textbook first so that you will know what questions to ask. You will get tired and angry, but keep at it. Your investment of time and energy will bring great dividends.

All during the process, affirm positive attitudes and obedience. Applaud every sign of progress, and think of creative ways to reward good grades. Making school a priority begins with you and the amount of time you give to this project.

INVOLVED PARENTS

Despite the flurry of interest in the field, relatively few parents stay involved with their children's education through high school. . . .

Research by Search Institute and others finds that family or parent involvement has a significant impact on students' well-being and success in school.

When parents are involved in school, students tend to have higher levels of commitment to their own education. A recent analysis of parent involvement by Search Institute for the General Mills Foundation found that sixth- and twelfth-grade students with involved parents tend to be more motivated in school and more committed to continuing education beyond high school.

A Child Trends report found that sixth- and twelfth-grade students whose parents are highly involved in their education are less likely to experience various problems in school (*Running in Place: How American Families Are Faring in a Changing Economy and an Individualistic Society*, 1994). For example, twenty-six percent of students with highly involved parents are in the bottom half of their class, compared to fifty-six percent of those whose parents are minimally involved. And eleven percent of youth with highly involved parents have repeated a grade, compared to twenty-five percent of those whose parents are minimally involved. Indeed, some research suggests that parent involvement is a more powerful predictor of student behavior than family income.

—*Source*[1]

Involvement

Another important but difficult choice is to become involved in your teens' schools. When children are young, parents flock to the elementary school programs, fun fairs, open houses, and teacher conferences. As kids get older, however, parental involvement tapers off. Perhaps parents don't know how to get involved in junior high schools and high schools. Maybe they are intimidated by the older kids. Perhaps they just assume that their teenagers don't want them around anymore. Or they may think that the schools are closed to them. Whatever the reason, they stay away from the campus.

I have found, however, that junior high and senior high teachers and administrators want and welcome parents to their campuses. The schools still have annual open houses and parent-teacher conferences. That's the place to begin your involvement, to meet the teachers and familiarize yourself with the building. At open houses, when you follow the abbreviated schedule and go to your teenagers' classes, introduce yourself to each teacher. Then sign up for a personal conference where you can discuss your teens' study habits and grades.

Junior high and middle schools provide many other opportunities for parents to get involved with students. Teachers are always looking for parent sponsors and volunteers to help with fundraising, chaperoning, transportation, office work, and a host of other jobs. One of my neighbors has helped to build the sets for the middle school and high school musicals for the past several years. He enjoys helping, and the drama and musical directors really appreciate his work. One year I served as an overnight chaperone for an "outdoor education" trip. I didn't get much sleep, but I learned about the school and got to know several kids. And for seven years, a shop teacher and I led the Campus Life/JV club on Fridays before school.

High schools also offer many opportunities for parental involvement. At our daughters' school, parents assist with sports activities and run the Booster Club, the Music Parents Association, the Home and School Association, and other clubs. Parents also serve as tutors and career mentors. In addition, every year the principal organizes his Principal's Parent Council, to which he invites all who want to come. Your teenagers' high school will have similar opportunities. Find the ones that fit you and get involved. Even if you can't find time to immerse yourself in a volunteer organization, you can support the school by attending the games, concerts, and special events.

Your involvement in your children's schools will demonstrate your commitment to their education and to the school system itself.

DRAWING MORE
We need more parental involvement. . . . The kids of the parents who are most involved are the successful students. So if we could find ways to draw more parents into school life, the students would be better off. We need more parents going to PTA and feeling comfortable calling the teachers or coming into the building for conferences to check on the students.

—Sylvia Skarstad
"View from the Chalkboard," Youthworker[2]

Balanced Life

Balance is important in life. Going to an extreme and over-emphasizing one area will result in serious neglect of the others. The caricature of the "dumb jock" provides a good example. While spending all of his time lifting weights and working out, this great physical specimen ignores his studies and other aspects of his life. Thus, while building his muscles, he may stunt his mental, social, and spiritual growth.

It is possible to be out of balance in other areas. Some teenagers immerse themselves in social activities, ignoring their health and grades. Others may run from church service to Bible study to youth group and never learn how to think or how to relate to people.

God created us as *whole* persons—physical, social, mental, and spiritual. And he wants us to be whole—healthy, developed, and mature. The Bible contains numerous challenges and guidelines for glorifying God in each area of life. We are to treat our bodies as temples of the Holy Spirit (1 Corinthians 6:19-20); we are to study and renew our minds (2 Timothy 2:15; Romans 12:2); we are to love and care for others (1 Corinthians 13; 1 John 4:7); we are to grow spiritually (1 Peter 2:2). And in all we do, we are to keep God at the center (Matthew 6:33), do our best (Colossians 3:23), glorify God (1 Corinthians 10:31), reflect Christ (Matthew 5:16), and share God's Good News (1 Peter 3:15).

FAMILY STUDY TIME

The best dad I know did two things to encourage his kids academically. First, he made a rule that the television would never be turned on during the weekdays. Second, he instituted a "family study time" every evening. While the boys did their homework, he and his wife read or prepared for an upcoming Bible study. The boys were taught that learning is not just for kids—it is a lifelong pursuit.
—Len Woods
Minister to Students, Christ Community Church,
Ruston, Louisiana

Help your teenagers maintain balance. While some of you have teenagers who are out of balance because they are too busy, many of you deal with children who need to value the education that comes from a healthy involvement with classes and extra-curricular activities. Encourage them to get involved in school beyond classes and homework.

As you help your adolescents stay balanced, remember to maintain your balance. Don't demand and push your teens to do *everything*. But if your teenagers tend to do *nothing*, be the outside force that breaks through the inertia. Help them find physical outlets—an interscholastic or intramural sport, a work-out schedule, aerobics—and work with them to develop healthy lifestyles. Direct your teenagers to social functions such as clubs, school organizations, and youth groups. And encourage your teens to explore the arts—music, drama, art, creative writing. They may surprise both you and themselves by finding a hidden interest or latent talent.

Outreach

Through all of this, work at developing a spiritual sensitivity, a concern for reaching other kids for Christ. Your church youth group and other youth ministries will be invaluable allies in this effort (see chapter 3). Talk with your adolescents about their friends' needs and struggles, and pray about those kids together.

You also may want to plan a strategy together for reaching out to your teenagers' friends. In addition to praying for their friends, they could invite them to Campus Life, Young Life, Fellowship of Christian Athletes, or youth group meetings and events where they will have fun and hear the gospel. Winter ski trips and summer camps have proven to be very effective for reaching teenagers for Christ. When they are away from home and other distractions, young people are able to evaluate their lives honestly and think clearly about eternal issues. You may want to help your teens start a small group discussion or Bible study in your home.

Work with your kids to maximize this important time of their lives and the God-sent opportunities to share their faith.

* * *

Many young people see very little value in their classes and other school activities. But during the junior and senior high school years, they should be laying a solid foundation for their lives. In your home, choose to make education a top priority, to get involved in your teenagers' schools, to model and teach the balanced life, and to reach out with your teens to reach their friends for Christ.

THINK IT THROUGH

1. How much time do your teenagers spend on homework every night?
2. How do you feel about your kids' current academic performance?
3. What signs of inertia do you see in your teens?
4. What excuses do your kids give for not studying more or for not being more involved in school?
5. What will be your new rules for studying and for doing homework?
6. What can you do to help your teenagers with their schoolwork?
7. Where will each teen study?
8. In what ways will you become involved in your teens' schools?
9. What new classes or extracurricular activities may help your adolescents find their identity and build self-esteem?
10. What areas should your teenager develop in order to be more balanced?
11. For which of your teens' friends will you begin to pray regularly?
12. What can you and your teenagers do to reach their friends for Christ?

CHAPTER **8**

"But I Need Money"

*"Do you guys realize how much
work there is in having a paper
route? . . . You fellows have
started this job; I want you to
complete it and do a good,
thorough job."*
          —Ozzie to David and Ricky
             from "The Paper Route"

"WELL, WHAT DO you think, Marge? Should we let him take the job or not?" Seated in his favorite chair in the family room, Cliff Cordell looks up from his newspaper, turns to his wife, and awaits her response. Then he quickly adds, "I'm for it."

"Oh, I don't know, honey," Marge replies. "Johnny seems a little young for that. I mean, he only just turned sixteen. I know Mr. Larson is being very generous with his offer, but I'm afraid that work may interfere with school and church. I wish we had more time to think about this. Johnny just told us about the job at dinner, and Mr. Larson needs to have an answer tomorrow."

"Lots of kids work, Marge," Cliff responds. "I had jobs when I was a kid, and I turned out all right. Look at the Ferrano boy. He's now the assistant manager at CD World, and he's still in high school." Speaking with steadily increasing emotion, Cliff adds, "Besides the money, I think the job would teach John how to organize his finances and how to take responsibility. That's the problem with kids today; they're lazy and want everything done for them and given to them. They ought to pay their own way!"

Marge quickly interrupts, "Now, Cliff, let's not get carried away. It's not right to expect children to support the family. That's the parents' responsibility."

"I know, I know," Cliff answers. Then raising his voice slightly, he continues, "But John's not a child anymore. For heaven's sake, Marge, he's sixteen. It's about time he learned the value of a dollar and what the real world is all about. And this way he can get the car he's always talking about. The more we talk, the more I think this job offer is a great opportunity—a godsend!"

Marge Cordell sighs and then softly replies, "You may be right. I guess it's hard for me to accept the fact that Johnny is growing up." Pausing for a moment and then brightening, she adds, "Actually, with his own car, he won't have to depend on us so much, and we won't have to pay extra on our car insurance for him. That sure will help the family budget!"

"Then it's settled," Cliff states with a note of finality. He picks up the newspaper again. "I'll tell John as soon as he gets home from Julio's house. I think this will work out just fine."

* * *

Similar discussions occur regularly all over America, with conclusions similar to the one reached by Cliff and Marge Cordell. Young people are moving into the workplace, filling part-time and even full-time positions during their high school years. Some kids begin even earlier, working during junior high.

The Challenge

Many employers hire high school students for financial reasons. They can pay teenagers minimum wage, and they don't have to provide health insurance and other expensive benefits for part-time employees. Fast-food franchises, retail stores, restaurants, delivery services, and similar businesses offer many opportunities for unskilled laborers. With just a small cost for training, these employers risk very little by hiring young people. And some businesses skirt the system, avoiding taxes and government regulations by paying young employees in cash.

In the face of numerous employment opportunities, many teenagers are drawn into the workplace, motivated by materialism and independence and encouraged by peers and parents.

Materialism

Despite Cliff Cordell's assertion about what his son will learn about managing money and taking responsibility, the overwhelming motive for most working teens is financial, not educational. They want dollars in their pockets and in the bank because they desire to buy *what* they want, *when* they want it, without needing to ask their parents for money. Often these young people want to buy expensive things like a stereo, a new wardrobe, or an automobile.

We shouldn't be surprised that our kids look to money and possessions for happiness and fulfillment. The gospel of one of the gods of our age, materialism, is preached on television and radio, in films and videos, and in every magazine and newspaper. The American philosophy of life can be summarized by a popular bumper sticker: "The person who dies with the most toys wins." Very early in life, children develop this craving for material things—the hot toy, the popular doll, the basketball shoes, the latest fashion, the creative gadget. Advertisers, skilled at creating a thirst, market their products for the young and broadcast their appealing ads during Saturday-morning cartoons and other children's programs. And they heighten the thirst by using celebrities to endorse and hawk their wares.

Some parents unwittingly promote a materialistic outlook by spoiling their children, giving them almost everything they ask for, satisfying nearly every whim. It's easy to fall into this trap because good parents love their kids and want them to be happy. But true happiness can't be bought, and promoting the misconception that it can will eventually prove harmful. Teenagers who were spoiled as young children usually have little appreciation for the true value of money or possessions. They do not understand the purpose of money, how to budget their funds, or how to control their spending.

Other parents contribute to an unrealistic financial perspective through their own selfish spending habits. Tight with money for children and family yet spending freely on themselves—new car, latest computer upgrade, home entertainment system, country club membership, vacation cruise, latest fashions, tickets to professional athletic contests—they model a shallow, self-centered philosophy of financial responsibility. As children in these homes grow older, they become eager to spend *their own* money on *themselves* too, just as their parents do. Parents also can send a negative message by referring to "my money." For example, a wife may say to her husband, "I bought this dress with *my* money, so don't bug me about it!"

Most kids learn and eventually reflect values their parents model. Quite naturally, American children learn to want *money*. And materialistic children grow into materialistic adolescents. These teenagers quickly determine that the quickest and easiest way to obtain their own spending money is to get a job that pays well but doesn't require too much time and effort. Most kids take jobs because they want the money, not because they want to work.

Independence

Some of the motivation to get a job and earn money arises from teenagers' push for independence. Undoubtedly the greatest contemporary symbols of independence are money and cars. Consider the automobile advertisements on television. Almost all highlight the freedom of the road. In addition, credit card, bank, and lottery ads promote the idea that money brings power and independence: with enough money, a person can *be* anything, *do* anything, and *have* anything that he or she desires. And most high school juniors and seniors have friends or acquaintances who seem to fit that image: the girl with the credit card, the boy with the new car, and so forth.

Money leads to independence.

Peer Influence

For some teenagers, peer pressure is the dominant factor in their push to get a job. Many of their friends work and thus have the money and the independence that money brings. These friends may invite them to shop, ski, eat out, and do other activities that require money. Kids without the funds can't participate.

Also, some high school friends have their own cars and seem to drive everywhere. Having one's own wheels seems very appealing to teens who always have to ask for rides.

Kids who don't have much money can feel left out of the group.

Parent Push

In addition to being pulled by materialism, independence, and friends, many teenagers are encouraged by their parents to work. This happens for several reasons:

1. Many parents are tired of hearing their teenagers ask for money or complain about not having enough when they want to buy CDs and clothes or go out with their friends. These parents hope to gain peace and have less hassle around the house with the teenagers working. So they may suggest employment by saying something like: "If you need so much money, you ought to get a job!" Others imply the same message through sarcasm: "If you had to work for your money, you'd appreciate it more and realize that it doesn't grow on trees!"

2. Some parents have much more self-centered motives. They know that if their teenagers earn their own income, they will need less parental financial support, which will ease the pressure on the family budget. Some parents even figure that they will have more

money to spend on themselves. For these parents, the sooner their teens can become self-supporting, the better.

3. Other moms and dads do not have adequate income and struggle to meet their financial needs. These families need every dollar they can get. Kids in these homes will have to pay their own way to college if they want to go. In extreme cases of poverty or in some single-parent families, the kids will need to work to help pay for the basic necessities, including food, rent, and clothes.

4. Still other parents sincerely believe that having a job will help their adolescents learn the value of work, marketable skills, how to handle and manage money, and other valuable lessons. These moms and dads feel that if kids have to work for their money, they will appreciate it more and thus will be careful about how they spend it. These adults may also look back at their own experience as working teens and remember lessons and skills that they learned on the job.

5. Hearing that other teenagers have jobs, some moms and dads may just figure that getting a job is normal and even expected. So they will offer employment suggestions: "Why don't you get a job like Sean's?" or "I know Gerald Morgan, who owns RiteWay Cleaners. Would you like me to contact him for you?"

Parents can add to the pressure to find a job, get to work, and earn money.

The Conflict
Many of the arguments for teenagers holding down jobs and earning their own money sound inviting. Certainly it is important

for young people to learn money-management skills: hard work, discipline, budgeting, spending, shopping, and saving. And who can dispute the relationship between money and independence? It is no wonder that joining the workforce holds great appeal. Unfortunately, however, that financial vision is largely an illusion. Instead of helping teens, steady employment can hurt them.

Taught to Waste

There is no doubt that employment brings money. Working teenagers have money to spend, sometimes lots of it. But instead of learning how to *save* and *manage* that money, most learn how to *waste* it. Suddenly they have cash in their pockets, dollars that they are free to spend on themselves. And they do just that. In fact, often these adolescents develop spending habits that are very difficult to break later in life. Money and self-centered spending can become habit forming.

Most teenagers who work have no bills or financial obligations. And if they do, usually it is just one—a car payment, for example. That distorts their picture of adult-level financial responsibility. Thus, their use of money gives them practice with the wrong set of habits—spending *most* of what they earn on what they want.

During my three decades of youth ministry, I have had contact with hundreds of students who held part-time or even full-time jobs while they were in high school. Of these working teenagers, I found very few who had learned to manage their money well and to discipline their spending. In addition to the walk-around-with-cash-in-the-pocket-spend-at-whim attitude, they also spent large amounts on clothes, cars, stereos, tapes, CDs, concerts, and other entertainment.

In my experience, most of the kids who work really don't have to take a job to support the family. That is, they come from middle-class homes well above the poverty level. Many, of course, are expected to save for college; some have to pay their whole way. I have known families who are struggling financially and need their kids to contribute to the family income. But even in these situations, where cash is scarce, I have seen working teens waste their money on themselves. And if you think they are learning the value of work and an appreciation for the job, look again. They change jobs often, quitting for the flimsiest excuses (had a date, didn't like the supervisor, wanted to take a trip with a friend, got tired of the work).

HOW KIDS USE MONEY

Teens are big spenders—to the tune of more than $1 billion each week. . . . Four categories of products—clothing, food, entertainment, and electronics—account for more than 80 percent of what they spend. Entertainment products, such as cassette tapes, CDs, and videocassettes, represent about 15 percent of teens' spending.

—George Barna
"Is Your Store Cool Enough?"[1]

Certainly there are exceptions to what I have just described; some kids really do work hard, save money, and spend responsibly. But research on teenage spending has borne out the fact that most tend to waste what they earn. I have seen this repeatedly in my own experience.

Fed a Lie

Tied closely to the problem of learning how to waste money is the subtle draw of materialism and greed, the idea that money and possessions can bring happiness. As we discussed earlier, this is a great illusion that our kids are believing more and more. One example of this is the growing gambling addiction among young people.[2] Looking for the quick hit, they buy the lottery tickets, bet on sporting events, or ride a riverboat hoping to gain instant riches. In many cases, parents or older friends will gamble for underage adolescents.

Added to this temptation to have money right away is the youthful misperception of time. For adolescents, a year seems like a very long time; five years can seem like forever. That's because five years is a large chunk of their lifetime. Thus teenagers struggle with patience. It's tough for them to wait for anything! They don't want to listen to adults who tell them to *prepare* for the future and *wait* for maturity. They want needs met, good feelings, fun, and pleasure *now!*

The lure of money, big money, is strong, enticing young people to mortgage their future for the possibility of making big bucks right away.

Pulled Away

The first casualties of young people working during the school year are extracurricular activities. Each day has a limited amount of time. Students attend classes for about seven hours, eat for another couple of hours, and sleep for about seven hours, leaving only eight hours for friends, homework, work, and activities. Apart from weekends, those available hours fall right after school and in the evenings, so that's when kids work. Sports, musical groups, plays, clubs, and other extracurricular activities have their practices, games, meetings, and performances at that time. So unless teenagers have very *part-time* jobs or special arrangements with the employer, they will not be able to work and be involved with extracurricular activities at the same time.

I'M GLAD I DIDN'T WORK

Despite the pressure that I needed to contribute several thousand dollars a year to my college education, I didn't work for pay during the high school academic months. My parents never forced me to work during those years. Instead they encouraged me to be involved in speech, music, drama, and the newspaper. They had the foresight to realize that those experiences would have a significant impact on my future—and they have. When school was out for the summer, though, I was expected to have a full-time job. Now that I am nearly finished with my university studies, I am grateful that my parents had that perspective. I never had the kind of pocket money some of my friends had—and still don't—but I feel that I had a balanced, well-rounded high school experience and a solid preparation for the future.

—Matt, twenty-year-old fourth-year university student

Even if the actual hours do not conflict, most working teens still will avoid extracurricular activities because of the overall pressure on their time. They would rather fill up their off-hours with socializing, shopping, and, perhaps, even studying.

Speaking of studying, that's the next activity to be eliminated from the working student's life. In addition to having less time for doing homework, many of these young people find that their lives increasingly focus on the job and their friends at work. Thus, school becomes less of a priority to them. Recently a high school principal told me that a student had requested a reduced school schedule, less than the legal requirement, so she could put in more hours on her job. When the principal asked why she needed to work, the girl explained that she wanted to buy a car. This girl's work is taking over her life.

Young people who neglect classes, homework, and extracurricular activities cheat themselves out of a great experience and limit their future. Instead of laying a solid educational founda-

NO TIME FOR HOMEWORK

Some disagree, but I think too many young people today have jobs. If they're asked, many teachers say the biggest problem is that half the kids don't have time for homework. Students tell me they don't have time for homework because "I have to work" or "I had to shut down the store last night." Some of them really must contribute to the family, but too many of them simply want the expensive clothing, the car . . . then they have to pay for the insurance. I think more of them work to pay for material things than to save for college. This seriously cheats them. They do not make nearly the kind of progress they could if school were a priority.

—Sylvia Skarstad
"View from the Chalkboard," *Youthworker*[3]

tion for a wide variety of career options in the future, they limit themselves to dead-end jobs that give them wanted cash today.

Working teenagers also curtail their involvement in church activities. Many have to work on Sundays, so they don't even make it to the worship services. Others pull out of the youth group and other Christian ministries because of time conflicts or studies or because their interests have shifted to the workplace. Adolescence is the critical time for faith development. Our kids need spiritual input.

In some extreme cases, the demands of a job become so great that youthful employees are left with very little time for family and friends. For whatever reason, some kids fill up every available hour with work, stopping off at home only to sleep, change clothes, and grab a bite to eat before heading out to school or to the job.

Work can pull teenagers away from school, church, and even family and friends.

Exposed

Many parents like the idea of their teenagers learning adult skills and responsibilities while they work. That may happen on some jobs, but in virtually every case, working teens learn more than their parents anticipated—the wrong lessons.

First, these kids are exposed to "adult" pressures from employers, customers, and the work itself. These job-related stresses can lead to "adult" physical problems including insomnia, stomach ulcers, and migraine headaches. Many of these by-products of stress can be more prevalent and more severe with young people than with adults because teens lack emotional maturity, life experience, and coping skills. Imagine the stress teenage employees experience when a customer ac-

CHALLENGE TO POPULAR WISDOM

The findings of recent research on youthwork constitute a challenge to popular wisdom and conventional belief. Some of the findings will surprise those who believe that hefty doses of work experience are a sure cure for an assortment of adolescent vagaries. Among the most striking of these discoveries are that extensive part-time employment during the school year may undermine youngsters' education; that working leads less often to the accumulation of savings or financial contributions to the family than to a higher level of luxury consumer spending; that working appears to promote, rather than deter, some forms of delinquent behavior; that working long hours under stressful conditions leads to increased alcohol and marijuana use; and— the *coup de grace*—that teenage employment, instead of fostering respect for work, often leads to increased cynicism about the pleasures of productive labor. Findings such as these lead us to conclude that the benefits of working to the development of adolescents have been overestimated, while the costs have been underestimated.

—Ellen Greenberger and Laurence Steinberg
When Teenagers Work [4]

cuses them of incompetence, when a supervisor places unreasonable demands on them, or when they have to handle unexpected crises.

Second, working teens are exposed to "adult" lifestyles. Studies have shown that young people who work tend to swear, drink, smoke, and use illegal drugs much more than young people who don't work. Researchers conclude that the main reason for this is the teenagers' association with coworkers who engage in these destructive behaviors. In addition to spending time with these people every day, they form friendships that often lead in a negative direction.

Work causes young people to "grow up" too fast.

Trapped

As mentioned earlier, many teenagers work in order to buy a car, a symbol of freedom and independence. Often these same teenagers will explain that they *need* a car for their work. But young people don't realize the expense. Automobiles cost a lot to buy and to maintain, and they strain and drain the finances. Insurance premiums, for example, can be very high for teenagers—well over a thousand dollars annually in some areas—and gas and repairs are not cheap. This becomes a vicious cycle: the more teenagers work, the more they use the car and the more they need to the money to support the driving habit. The car becomes a money pit. This way of life traps teens. Slavery to a job and a car is a terrible price to pay for freedom.

Besides the cost, another problem with teenagers having their own cars involves the speed at which they can be miles away from their parents, totally unsupervised. Of course that can happen whenever anyone drives any car. But kids are much more likely to get into trouble in their own cars. When they drive their parents' car, they don't use it quite as often, and they tend to be more careful. Getting a driver's license should not be the signal for buying a car. Young drivers need to ease into driving, gaining needed maturity and experience.

That highly valued automobile can be a deadly trap.

So, What's a Parent to Do?

What do we do when our teenagers want to have a job? Do we encourage them, hoping to decrease their drain on our family budget? Do we allow them to get a job and hope that they use their money wisely? Do we prohibit them from any job?

The Choice

As in other family situations, this whole issue of money and teenagers will require tough choices. Again, these choices will be difficult because they will seem to run counter to what our society and our adolescents' friends value and promote. But they are necessary if we want to help our kids grow and mature into responsible adults.

Model

Already I have written much about what parents' lifestyles communicate to their children. Believe it: kids pick up their parents' values. So evaluate your lifestyle to determine the values you are modeling for your children. Consider materialism and your attitude toward money. And where does your career fit in your list of priorities? Think of how your kids would answer if they were asked to list what you value the most.

It is easy to say that God and family stand at the center of life and that everything revolves around them. But the truth can be determined by examining where people invest their time, money, and emotions. Some parents put big bucks into a car or a computer and keep the kids and their friends in their place, a safe distance away. Some adults spend nearly every waking hour on the job or thinking about it. Some fix their gaze squarely on money, pinching pennies, complaining about bills, and working every angle to get more. Some moms and dads seem to worry much more about the house or a prized possession than about their children.

JUST LIKE US

While you wait for your teenagers to grow up, you can take comfort in the fact that by the time young people reach their mid-twenties, their lines are almost always identical to the lines their parents drew. So perhaps the point is not how we can get our kids to behave as we want them to, but how we can be the kind of parents we ought to be so that when our kids are like us, we'll like what they are.

—Jay Kesler
Energizing Your Teenager's Faith[5]

Materialism is catching; greed is contagious. Remember Paul's admonition to young Timothy: "People who want to get rich fall into temptation and a trap and into many foolish and harmful desires that plunge men into ruin and destruction. For the love of money is a root of all kinds of evil. Some people, eager for money, have wandered from the faith and pierced themselves with many griefs" (1 Timothy 6:9-10).

So the first tough choice involves your attitude toward money and your lifestyle. Let your children know by your attitudes and actions that money and possessions do *not* hold top spot in your life. Pray together about the finances during difficult times; talk together about tithing and supporting the church and other ministries; let the family know that you value people much more highly than things, even the shiny new car.

Jesus reminds us: "You cannot serve two masters: God and money. For you will hate one and love the other, or else the other way around" (Matthew 6:24, TLB).

Say No

The second tough choice is one that I am sure you anticipated throughout this chapter: Say no to the job; don't allow your teenager to work during the school year. I understand that in some cases young people have to work to support the family or to earn money for college. But even in those situations, keep the working hours minimal and make studies and extracurricular activities important. Many schools have partnerships with selected businesses and offer part-time employment as part of their course work, allowing students to combine work with school. That would be one way to keep work to a minimum.

Your teens will be working for most of their lives; don't start them early. Let them learn from and enjoy the teenage years.

If you and your adolescents decide that an after-school, part-time job is necessary, help your teenagers understand that the money earned is not exclusively theirs to spend as desired. This income, like the earnings you and your spouse make, should be considered "family money" and should be managed well to help the whole family.

The important thing to communicate here is that no one in the family is an isolated individual who lives completely for himself or herself. Each person relates to the others, and each person's actions affect the others. That's the nature of "family." Most teenagers have very little understanding of family financial matters. This would be a good time to explain how you and your spouse budget your income and expenses. Show how a spending choice in one area reduces the amount of money available to spend in another area. For example, you could decide to spend thousands of dollars on an expensive new car, but that would make it very difficult to pay for that first year of college. As responsible parents, you prioritize and then spend accordingly. Then explain that your children should have the same attitude toward finances, even money earned on part-time jobs. That is,

TOO QUICKLY PUSHED

We encourage our parents not to have their kids consider getting a job until maybe they're juniors or seniors. And if they do, it should be very, very part time. We notice that having jobs pushed them quicker into adulthood than we wanted them to be.

—David Olshine
Director of Youth Ministry, Columbia International University

they should be thinking of how their saving and spending habits affect the rest of the family, positively and negatively.

In college, I noted that a friend ate all his meals in the student union, despite the fact that his parents had paid for his meals in the dining hall. I asked him why he would pay extra for food when his meals had already been purchased. He answered that he didn't like the dining hall food, that he had a job, and that it was *his* money to spend as he pleased. This is the kind of self-centered, individualistic attitude to which I am referring. My friend's parents were sacrificing to send him to college, yet he was wasting money with the excuse that the money was "his."

I am not suggesting that you exercise your authority and simply take the paychecks. Instead, you should give your teenagers the responsibility and authority to control and to spend what they earn. But they should know that the money must be managed well and that you will be checking to make sure that happens. Help them set up spending records and savings plans, which I will discuss later in this chapter.

However, if your teens want to work during their school vacation weeks and during the summer months, that's a different matter. With no conflicts from school, your teenagers can be encouraged to work as much as possible, saving money for college and the future. Even at this time, however, check out the reputation of the employer, the working conditions, the type of work, and the hours for a typical work week. Don't fall for big-dollars-little-work opportunities. Usually these schemes promise much more than they deliver, and they may even be illegal. And be sure to keep Sundays open for worship, rest, and family.

Regardless of the pressure from your teenagers and their friends, don't give in. Say no to the job if possible. Also, encourage your teens to make schoolwork, extracurricular activities, and church involvement priorities.

Say Yes

It is not enough to prohibit your teenagers from working; you should also look for ways to say yes. This begins with spending.

One of the strong pushes for a job is to earn money for personal use. In addition to giving a weekly allowance, look for ways to *employ* your teenagers around the house. This work should be in addition to the regular jobs assigned to each family member. Often called "chores," these assignments are small, daily or weekly tasks needed to ensure the smooth running of the household. Chores can include setting the table, vacuuming the carpets, mowing grass, shoveling snow, raking leaves, ironing clothes, walking the dog, and

THE EFFECT ON GRADES

While there is little evidence to suggest that students who do less well in school are more likely to become workers during the high school years, there is indirect evidence that they work longer hours than other youngsters. There is also some evidence to suggest that grade point average is depressed by intensive levels of labor-force participation, especially among youth who begin work early in the high school years. Although the relationship between working and GPA does not always attain statistical significance, it is consistently negative. In no studies has working been shown to have a positive effect on GPA.

—Ellen Greenberger and Laurence Steinberg
When Teenagers Work[6]

so forth. Every child needs to contribute some time and energy to the family. And every child needs an allowance, a minimal amount of money given as a *share* of the family finances. The allowance is not a wage or pay. Kids don't *earn* it; they receive the money because they belong to the family. There is no right amount to give as an allowance for a particular age or for all families. Selecting the amount involves considering many factors. Just remember, however, that it is much easier to *increase* the amount than to decrease it—so begin conservatively. You may, for example, give a seventh grader five dollars a week. Then you could add a dollar or two per week each year.

For extra work, however, you can hire your kids and then pay them generously for their efforts. Special jobs could include planting bushes, painting the fence, building a doghouse, steam cleaning the carpets, painting or wallpapering a room, changing the oil in the car, cleaning out the garage—any task that you may employ someone else to do. In addition, kids can still earn money through baby-sitting, mowing lawns, and shoveling snow in the neighborhood.

Also, keep an open wallet when possible for paying for school field trips, club dues, music, and sports equipment. Because your teenagers have very little outside source of income, don't expect them to pay for every school expense. This will cost you a bit more than perhaps you thought, but that is better than the alternative.

Saying yes also involves compromising and sharing, especially when it comes to the family automobiles. Work out a plan so that your teenage driver can use a car to take friends to a game or activity, to go on a date, or just to drive to school. This may mean that *you* hitch a ride with a friend to choir practice and let your daughter take the car to club volleyball practice instead of the other way around. In fact, use of the car can be a motivational and disciplinary tool; for example, allowing your son to drive his friends to the Campus Life meeting may overcome his inertia and get him going.

Some families, especially those who have more than one teenager and who can afford it, buy another car for the kids to use. This helps ease the strain on the other cars as well as the scheduling and chauffeuring stress. Even in this case, teenagers should know that this is a *family* car that they are using. Although they have the primary responsibility for upkeep, maintenance, and gas, the automobile belongs to the family and may be used by other members from time to time.

Look for ways to say yes to your teens' desire for cash and the car. It will keep you involved in their lives and will weaken the push for a job. Allowing teenagers to use the family automobiles may inconvenience their parents, but that will be far better than having the expense and problems of owning their own cars.

Teach

Regardless of the amount or source of their funds, kids need to be taught how to budget and how to spend their money. Even young children can be taught how to divide their allowance into budget categories like "God," "Saving," and "Spending." Some families use the jar or envelope system, with a container designated for each category. At allowance time, 10 percent can be put

SAVING?

Over eighty percent of high school seniors who work save "none" or only "a little" of their earnings. Money earned and saved during the later years of high school could be used, of course, to offset the costs of further education and to help establish an independent household. The failure of youngsters to save, therefore, can be viewed as a loss of assets for making the transition to adulthood.

—Ellen Greenberger and Laurence Steinberg
When Teenagers Work[7]

aside for "God," 10 to 20 percent for "Saving," and the rest for "Spending." As kids get older, you can add categories. The Campus Life/JV program uses a helpful acronym: GSSS, which stands for *Giving* (to God and to people in need), *Saving* (money in the bank for a big expense in the future, such as college or a special trip), *Stashing* (for a special purchase or need in the near future, such as a radio, or camp registration), and *Spending* (for buying day-to-day stuff). During a family meeting, explain how you as parents budget your money and how your income is spent. This will help everyone in the family understand and appreciate financial responsibility.

High school juniors and seniors can open checking accounts and begin to learn how to use a bank. Some parents give their older teens their portion of the clothes budget for a season or year and allow them to buy all their clothes. This helps them learn how to shop for the best values.

When your teenagers want an expensive item, talk it through with them. Help them to ask important questions. Do they really need the item? Is this purchase the *best* use of that money, or would it be better spent for something coming in the future? Be open to answering those questions about *your* purchases as well. And let your kids know that most of your purchases are the result of *decisions* you make, not the fact that you happen to have the money available. For example, a child may ask about buying a big-screen television set. Instead of answering that the set is too expensive and you can't afford it, explain that you have *chosen* to spend that amount of money on other, more important purchases (food, clothes, family vacation, college fund, or whatever).

Also, do not hide all your financial struggles from your kids. Don't frighten them by implying that you are nearly destitute. But when things are tight, ask for their prayers and help. Explain that the family will have to make some adjustments in lifestyle but that you will try hard to find the money for the important purchases and activities. Again, emphasize to the children that in many respects *all* the family's income belongs to the family and not to the individuals earning it. Part of what it means to be a family is family members sharing what they have with each other.

Through all of this discussion about money and possessions, be sure to teach the biblical principle of stewardship. In reality, we don't *own* anything—all we have belongs to God. Instead, we are caretakers, stewards, investors of what God has entrusted to us. Thus, it is up to us to be faithful and to do the best we can with all of God's resources (time, talent, and treasure). See

Matthew 25:14-30 for a discussion of the importance of wisely using what God has provided.

See the times when your teenagers need and ask for money as *teachable moments*. Take advantage of their desire and motivation by teaching them invaluable lessons about budgeting, spending, saving, and stewardship.

* * *

As kids grow older, they feel increasing pressure to have money, transportation, and independence. Usually they think that the quickest way to have all three is through a job. Don't fool yourself into believing that employment will teach your teenagers the value of money and how to manage it. Instead, having a job and ready cash often teaches the opposite and brings a host of other problems. Hold the line. Say no to work while kids are in school. But say yes to helping them get spending money and use of the car. Use these opportunities to teach them about responsible financial planning.

THINK IT THROUGH

1. Do teenagers you know work during the school year? Why do those students have jobs?
2. What in your lifestyle and speech may encourage your teenagers to be materialistic?
3. What motivates or may motivate your teenagers to get a job?
4. In what ways would your teens' studies, extracurricular activities, and church activities suffer if they were to take a job after school and on weekends?
5. Why do your teenagers want more money?
6. What can you do to help them get more?
7. What can your family members do to hold each other accountable for financial responsibility?
8. What changes should you make in your spending and saving habits to be a better steward of God's finances?
9. What compromises can you make regarding use of the family automobiles?
10. What can you do to teach your family the principles of biblical stewardship?

CHAPTER 9

"I Don't Wanna Do Sports Anymore"

"I'm surprised at you guys. You can't go through the rest of your lives being mad at people just because they don't arrange things to suit you."
—Ozzie to David and Ricky from "That Goshdarn Thornberry"

AWKWARD, EMBARRASSING SILENCE fills the kitchen as everyone turns toward Sharon. A few moments earlier, animated conversation had bounced across the table between bites of hamburger and corn. But now Luke, Zach, and their parents patiently await Sharon's answer. Larry Smith had asked about volleyball and how everything had gone the first day of tryouts. He and everyone else expected Sharon to answer with a cheery "Great!" and then fill them in on the details—the running, serving, hitting, and agility drills. Instead, Sharon looked down at the table and said nothing. She picks at the corn and lettuce strewn across her plate, breaking the silence with only the light clinks of fork on china.

"I asked you a question, Sharon," says Larry. "How were tryouts today?"

"I didn't go," Sharon mumbles, casting a quick glance upward at her father.

"What?" her dad replies, not believing his tenth-grade daughter's words. "Are you saying that you didn't try out?"

"Yes," Sharon answers softly, afraid to look at him. "There were so many girls in the gym, and besides, I really don't like it anymore, and—"

"But I thought you *loved* volleyball!" her dad breaks in. "In fact, you said it was your favorite sport. What happened?"

Sharon continues to try to explain her reasons. After a few follow-up questions and a brief lull in the conversation, the attention shifts to Luke and his day.

Later, Larry and Charlene Smith discuss Sharon's decision. "Sometimes I just don't understand that girl," begins Larry. "She changes her mind so quickly! I don't know if you heard her the way I did, Char, but it sounded as if she was afraid of the competition. What do you think we should do? I mean, this was only the first day. I'm sure she can still try out tomorrow. Maybe you should talk with her. I guess I just don't understand girls."

"It's not *that* bad, Larry," replies Charlene. "Let's not make too big a deal over volleyball. It's just a game. We should be thankful. Sharon is a good kid—she's not into drugs or anything like that. Anyway, remember, Sharon just turned fifteen. She needs to be making her own decisions. Maybe later she will miss volleyball and wish she were on the team and—"

"But then it will be too late," interrupts Larry. "Girls who don't play sophomore year never make it the next year. She's kissing volleyball good-bye!"

Larry and Charlene Smith are struggling with a dilemma many parents face, watching their teenagers drop out of extracurricular activities and seeing the years and opportunities slip by. Two years ago, Sharon stopped taking piano lessons. And as a freshman she seemed to lose interest in music altogether, so she didn't sign up for chorus this semester. Now she is pushing aside sports.

Sharon is typical of many young people who for a variety of reasons coast through junior high and high school. Involved in very few activities, they effectively bury their talents or allow their abilities to remain hidden.

The Challenge

As we have discussed in several chapters, adolescence brings change and discovery. Early adolescents experience cataclysmic transformation in nearly every area of life: physical, social, spiritual, emotional, and mental. These changes can confuse kids as they begin to doubt their abilities and identity: the former playground speedster who gained thirty pounds since fifth grade and whose feet have grown before his legs now feels clumsy and slow;

the "cute little girl" who has shot up to be a five-foot-eight-inch seventh grader now feels like an ugly giant; the fourth-grade math whiz who as an eighth grader cannot understand algebra feels like a failure. Many high school students have abandoned the dreams they held in elementary school—dreams of achieving greatness in academics, sports, or the arts.

At the same time that adolescents are going through these intense changes, they are inundated with information about themselves and the world through classes, news media, personal experiences, and close relationships. They are tested, encouraged, pushed, probed, timed, surveyed, and questioned as no previous generation in history has been evaluated. Educational options stretch to the horizon: camps, clinics, leagues, lessons, clubs, classes, performances, and productions. Recently, my high school daughter received tryout notices for a dozen volleyball clubs in our area (the clubs cost about one thousand dollars each, and all of them fill up very fast). And every season, parents form long lines to enroll children in our community's park district activities. The programs include cheerleading clinics, ice skating lessons, sports leagues, art classes, drama groups, computer seminars, and many more.

This information avalanche cuts both ways. Positively, it can help kids learn about themselves, providing children and parents with knowledge of new activities and with insight into aptitudes and abilities. Negatively, however, the information can seem overwhelming and confusing, and the schedule can become exhausting, causing kids to want to opt out altogether.

Burnout

I know teenagers who have played soccer every fall and spring since first grade. Quite frankly, instead of developing a love for the sport, many have tired of it. So they quit in mid-season or decide not to try out next time. This can happen with almost any activity into which a child has been pushed at an early age.

Other teens have grown too fast (causing them to be awkward) or not fast enough to stay with peers in the sport. They find it increasingly difficult to keep up with teammates; practices and even games turn from fun to hard work. I have seen this with soccer, basketball, gymnastics, baseball, and dance. The activity becomes drudgery, and these children don't enjoy it any more.

Some kids quit because they are burned out.

Laziness

Let's face it, many teens are just plain lazy. That is, they do not want to do the hard work necessary to become good at something. Perhaps it is just human nature to take the easy route, but that attitude seems epidemic among teenagers. Playing the piano was novel and fun until the teacher insisted on an hour of practice every day. The glory of being a basketball star seemed very appealing until the coach insisted that the team run a mile of sprints at every practice. The tomatoes, corn, and watermelons pictured on the packets of seeds looked mouthwatering until the ground had to be prepared. Adolescents hit harsh reality when they learn that good results come from good work.

This lazy tendency springs partly from their age. Children have a very unrealistic view of life and tend to take for granted the good things, assuming that food, clothing, and shelter come easily. Eventually, these young people may learn that money must be *earned* in order to buy what they need to live. But until they understand the necessity of working hard to achieve a goal, most kids have to be pushed and supervised in their labor.

Also, for many years teenagers have been fed television commercials that imply that they can soar above the basketball rim by wearing the right shoes, that they can snag a dream date by chewing the right gum, and that they can be wealthy beyond imagination by buying a lottery ticket. In reality, basketball proficiency, successful relationships, and financial independence result from work—hard work. But kids who believe what they see on television may think that the desired payoffs come easily and quickly.

Many teenagers pull out because the activities involve work.

Insecurity

A poor self-concept also causes many teens to withdraw from music, drama, sports, and other activities. A girl may have been praised for her beautiful singing voice in elementary school and may have seen herself as a singer. In high school, however, when she compares her singing with that of kids from other parts of town and kids whose voices have matured sooner, she may feel very average. This also can happen in sports, where children who have grown earlier than their peers get the attention and the starting positions on the junior high school athletic teams. A couple of years later in high school, however, these former seventh-grade stars may be riding the bench because their classmates have had their growth spurts, have caught up physically, and now are bigger, stronger, and faster.

This can become a vicious cycle: a girl who believes that she is not good at a sport probably won't perform well and thus will reinforce her idea that she is a poor player. At a summer camp, one of the boys on my team kept telling me that he was terrible at softball. Despite my words of encouragement, each time he went to bat, the boy would just stand there and take pitches or make halfhearted attempts to swing at the ball. Then, after striking out, he would walk slowly back to the bench, turn to me, and say, "See, I told you I wasn't any good."

In addition to the differences in maturity and physical size, a number of other factors can cause kids to suffer from low self-esteem:

FAILURE FEAR

How teens respond to challenges is closely related to their self-esteem and fear of failure. If they are burying their talents, they probably are afraid of failure and of disappointing their parents, others, and themselves. The bottom line for parents is to communicate constantly that you love them. Period. You love them for who they are, not for what they do.

—Kara Eckmann
Director of College Ministry, Lake Avenue Church, Pasadena

- *Ridicule.* Mocking words from a friend or acquaintance can make teenagers feel self-conscious and inferior.
- *Failure.* After a mistake, a poor performance, or a bad grade, adolescents can infer that they are failures or "stupid."
- *Intimidation.* Kids with an air of assurance and who walk and speak with confidence can be intimidating to teens who are not very sure of their abilities.
- *Comparison.* Young people can feel defeated before they begin by comparing themselves to others whom they assume are more skilled.
- *Lack of success.* Members of a losing team can feel like losers, especially when they lose repeatedly.
- *Expectations.* The inability to reach unrealistically high standards set by parents or the teens themselves can make them feel like failures.

Adolescents with low self-esteem will be reluctant to participate in a sport, try out for a play, take a special class, or join a group where they think that they will be doomed to fail or be rejected.

Discouragement

Kids who *do* try out and then don't make the team or get the part in the play can feel discouraged and defeated. After a couple of cuts, many of those kids do not want to try out again. Having hopes dashed can be very painful.

Whether it's from burnout, laziness, insecurity, or discouragement, many teens decline involvement in all extra activities, choosing, instead, to spend time with friends, in front of the television, or playing computer games.

The Conflict

On the surface, it could seem that there is no conflict here. After all, what is wrong with *not* participating in an organized sport, trying out for a musical or play, joining a club, attending a seminar, or taking lessons? Nothing. After all, participation is not required for becoming a Christian, maturing physically, graduating from high school, or being a good citizen. And it would be absurd to think that *every* child should take advantage of *every* special opportunity. Also, as we have discussed thoroughly in chapter 6, some teenagers try to do it all . . . to their peril.

The Problems

The problems occur when adolescents withdraw completely from almost *all* extracurricular activities. They deprive themselves of life-enriching experiences and self-discovery. As kids join, practice, and compete, they can begin to learn their limits and liabilities, and they can develop interests and skills.

Also, by dropping out, they may develop the habit of taking the easy way through life and settling for mediocrity.

Self-discovery. New parents rock their precious babies to sleep and dream of what they will become, envisioning bright futures in the arts, government, science, business, Christian work, and a host of other careers. Gazing at his young son's broad shoulders, a loving father may imagine an all-pro linebacker, or looking at his daughter's long fingers, he may see a future concert pianist. At that stage of life, the hopes and ideals are limitless: valedictorian, Miss America, Pulitzer Prize winner, Grammy-winning songwriter, president of the United States! Then, as the child grows, the parents adjust their dreams and begin to think in more realistic terms.

For any dreams to become reality, however, both child and parents need to have a basic understanding of the child's aptitudes, interests, and potential. These can be discovered through exposure to new experiences and information and through participation in special activities.

I grew up in a musical home. My parents sang duets together, and they loved music. So we sang as a family at various church functions, at homes on Christmas eve, in the choir, and at other occasions. Also, my mom played the violin, my dad directed the church choir, and all of us children took piano lessons. That exposure to music helped develop my interest and revealed a measure of musical talent. Thus, in junior high school and senior high school, I sang in choirs, performed in musicals, formed quartets and gospel teams, and sang solos. Music continues to hold an important place in my life. Without that early exposure to music, I doubt that I would have worked at developing and using my talent.

Currently, I am president of the Choir Parents Association of the local high school and thus have an inside look into our school's fine music department. Every year, many students awaken to their musical talent through their involvement in choir, band, or orchestra and through the encouragement, tutelage, and affirmation of the outstanding directors.

I have observed the same phenomenon in sports. Over the past ten years or so, I have coached youth soccer, basketball, and softball and even a couple of seasons of high school football. Each time, I would witness young people discovering an ability and love for the game. This story could be repeated by countless coaches and teachers of dance, drama, speech, art, computer science, writing, and a wide variety of other interests.

DISCOVERY

I advise parents to get their teens involved in some sort of mission or service opportunity. There, kids don't need all the honed skills necessary to meet the demands of school and academics. They feel accepted just the way they are.

On a mission or service opportunity, the real value is found in the giving of one's heart; it has very little to do with who a kid is or even his or her talents. Teenagers can discover much about themselves and see that giving is more important than receiving. They also learn that they can make a contribution that really makes a difference to the world.

I also encourage parents to allow their teens to become involved with people in socioeconomic levels that are different from their own. When a middle-income, suburban kid becomes involved with a low-income, urban kid, something sparks, and a connection is made. In this process, kids are able to evaluate their own cultures and values systems. This may be threatening to parents (some kids may return condemning middle-class lifestyles), but it will provide opportunities for the parents to discuss with their teens and build lasting value into their teenagers' lives.

—Ridge Burns
Director, Center for Student Missions

Teenagers who participate in activities such as those just mentioned can learn much about themselves. Those who drop out or refuse to become involved miss out on exciting self-discovery.

Good Habits. In addition to providing insight into teenagers' talents, abilities, and potential, involvement in clubs, on teams, and in activities can teach participants valuable lessons. For example, athletes can learn teamwork and control; musicians can learn persistence and poise; actors can learn communication skills. All participants can learn discipline as they practice hard to improve their techniques, refine their skills, and reach their goals. Discipline learned in academic pursuits and in these special activities carries over into other areas of life. Studies have shown that teenagers involved in extracurricular activities very likely will grow into responsible employees, spouses, church members, parents, and citizens. They will get involved, work hard, and keep their promises.

On the other hand, kids who drop out when the going gets tough (or who don't join because the activity or practice looks difficult) pick up bad habits. They learn to ignore their commitments and to take the easy way through life. Make no mistake, quitting can become almost habitual. Kids who quit the team, the club, the office, the staff, or the organization in the middle of the season, term, or performance will find it easier to quit again. Eventually, as adults, they may not think twice about leaving a job, breaking a contract, or dissolving a marriage during tough times. Quitting can become a habit—a lifestyle.

Self-esteem. As we have discussed earlier, the psychological-emotional focus for early adolescents is competence; that is, these kids have the need to find out what they are good at and to succeed at something. That motivates many young teens to try out and sign up for every activity announced at school. In addition, this emphasis on competence explains why junior high is the ideal time to teach kids skills, especially life skills.

We have also seen that the focus for middle adolescents is identity; that is, high school students have the need to find out who they are and where they fit. Obviously, failure in a class, in a sport, or in another activity may lead to a poor self-concept. But success, even limited success, can build self-esteem.

In competitive activities, the potential for failure is much greater than in activities where everyone can "win." In a choir, for example, all the members work together to perform a musical piece, and individuals are not put down or "benched" because they don't sing as well as others. Also, many clubs and campus organizations need members who simply have desire and give effort. And with one-on-one lessons, no one but the teacher, the student, and his or her parents knows how the student is progressing.

Teenagers can feel good about themselves and their abilities through their participation. Those who drop out or who don't get involved miss out on the opportunity to develop positive images of themselves.

The Parents

Many parents see their children's potential in music, academics, and sports, but they allow the kids to opt out. These parents don't want to pressure their teens into taking lessons or joining teams for a number of what would appear to be good reasons.

- *Conflict avoidance.* Some parents simply fear making their teenagers angry, especially when these kids have resisted their attempts to push them into activities in the past. Tired of all the arguments and hassles, they decide that it is just not worth the effort. At the first sign of resistance to a proposed activity, these parents drop it and just hope the kids will get involved in *something*. And they don't bring up the subject again.

- *Sensitivity.* Other moms and dads remember being pushed aggressively by *their* parents in directions that they didn't want to go. They remember reacting very negatively and thinking, "I'll never do that to my kids!" Pop psychology often mixes with these somewhat painful memories. Communicated through magazines, television talk shows, and neighbors, this message states that parents should be careful not to damage tender egos by "forcing" children to do anything. Instead, each child should be allowed to seek his or her own way in the world. Wanting to be sensitive to the special needs and desires of their children, these mothers and fathers give very little guidance to their teenagers and support few outside activities.

- *Free choice.* Some parents believe that children, especially teenagers, should make their own decisions as much as possible and thus should not be steered in any direction, certainly not against their will. These well-meaning parents may be motivated by an understanding of middle adolescents' move toward independence, or they may want their kids to know "reality discipline" (experiencing the results of their choices). Whatever the underlying reasons, these moms and dads allow their adolescents to choose nearly *all* of their extra activities.

Certainly these reasons sound legitimate. Few people enjoy conflicts, and every parent should be sensitive to a child's needs, desires, and developmental issues. But refusing to give direction, allowing kids to drift and to choose entirely their own way, is patently irresponsible. That would be like allowing infants to choose their diet, toddlers to choose their places to explore (including electrical outlets and hot stoves), or five-year-olds to choose their course of study. As with the children in these examples, middle school students are *not* mature enough to make all their decisions, especially those that will dramatically influence their future.

The above reasons are also unbiblical. God's Word strongly teaches that his people should be good stewards of his resources. These resources include the earth, our time, our money and possessions, and our very lives. God calls us to invest well what he has entrusted to us (see Matthew 25:14-30), to work hard at everything we do (see Colossians 3:23), to glorify God by the way we live (see 1 Corinthians 10:31 and 1 Peter 4:11), and to reach out to others with love and with the gospel (see John 13:34-35, 1 Corinthians 13, Matthew 28:19-20, and Acts 1:8).

Thus, as responsible Christian parents, we should do all we can to help our teenagers discover their talents, abilities, gifts, and potentialities so that they can contribute to society and make a difference for Christ in the world.

So, What's a Parent to Do?

In this area, choices are tough, not because we parents don't know *what* to do but because we don't know *when* to do it or *how much* to do. Just as it would be wrong to abdicate our parental responsibility and allow our kids to slide through life, it also would be wrong to go to the other extreme and push, prod, and pressure them to be conformed to our image of what they should be or become. We know that at times we should push and insist, but we don't want to overdo it. The right course of action falls somewhere in the middle.

The Choice

Unfortunately, I have no easy answers to this dilemma. But I do have guidelines that you can follow. Before reviewing the guidelines, however, it is important to consider the following principles.

- *You know your teenagers better than anyone else does.* Parents observe, nurture, and discipline their children from infancy and provide for all their needs. They stand as eyewitnesses to each child's first step, first word, first song, first day of school, first big failure, first great victory, and first love.

Thus, as you think back over the years, as if paging through a picture album, you remember snapshots of the whole range of your teens' experiences: vacations, tears, games, recitals, birthday parties, Christmas celebrations, award ceremonies, church services, and so many more. You have seen trends and tendencies, likes and dislikes, and hopes and disappointments. Thus you have a pretty good idea of what your teenagers need, what activities they would enjoy, and what lessons and experiences would benefit them most.

- *You have your own needs and dreams.* As we discussed earlier, many parents seek to meet their unfulfilled desires through their children. Mothers who wanted to be in the popular crowd when they were in high school may dress their daughters in designer clothes and encourage them to be cheerleaders. Fathers who identify intensely with professional athletes and vicariously win and lose with the home team may buy their young sons athletic equipment and insist that they play organized sports from their earliest days.

Having unfilled desires isn't wrong or sinful. If parents look back honestly at their teenage years, most of them will be able to identify several stillborn wishes in grades, sports, popularity, dating, Christian living, and extracurricular activities. Trouble occurs, however, when these parents pressure their teens, regardless of what those kids really need. Parents like these *use* their teenagers and do not act in their best interests. It is important, therefore, to evaluate your actions in light of your needs. When you push your teens, ask, "Whose needs am I meeting?"

- *You need help.* Although parents know their adolescents better than anyone else does, it still helps to have the insight of other adults who have contact with the kids and know them well. Teachers, coaches, youth leaders, pastors, school counselors or social workers, neighbors, relatives, and other adult friends can provide valuable insight to parents and their teens.

Identify the significant adults in your teenagers' lives. You and your spouse still will have to make the final decisions about your kids' activities, but you should get all the information you can from others who care about you and your family.

* * *

Keeping those principles in mind, here are guidelines for making the tough choices about your teenagers' activities as they learn from their involvement and prepare for the future.

Discover Your Teens' Unique Abilities

Every child is a special creation of our loving God and has a unique mix of personality factors, strengths, weaknesses, talents, abilities, and gifts. Thus each teen's expression of his or her special identity will be unique to that young person. No two kids are alike, not even siblings. And remember, not everyone is cut out to vault into a handstand on the balance beam or to lead the high school team to the championship in the math olympics or to build a china cabinet. So be careful about assuming that your teenager will be exactly like you, your spouse, or a sibling. And please don't expect your teenagers to keep up with a neighbor's children or with a cousin.

Instead, use your knowledge of your adolescents to help you determine where they may fit in and which activities may benefit them the most. If a son does well in art, steer him to another art

I WISH MY PARENTS HAD PUSHED ME

When I was in middle school, my parents encouraged me to be in the orchestra. They even offered to give me private lessons. But I resisted. I was large for my age, and I thought that being in the orchestra would make me a wimp. But now that I am a sophomore in high school, I regret that I did not study the violin. I wish my parents had pushed harder. They saw in me something that went beyond what my life was like in seventh grade. They saw a love for music and an ability to express myself through music. In some ways it's too late to learn to play the violin. Most of my classmates are quite proficient already. But maybe when I'm adult, I'll consider it again.

—Terry, sixteen-year-old male high school student

class in school. If a daughter shows an interest in music, look for ways to help her explore that interest.

At this point, the other adults in your teens' lives can provide valuable counsel. Ask teachers for an honest appraisal of your kids' ability and potential in a specific course of study; ask coaches for insight into athletic strengths and weaknesses; ask youthworkers for hints about your teenagers' hopes and dreams.

The better you know your children, the better you will be able guide them.

Insist on Involvement . . . Somewhere

When kids have a bad experience in an activity, they want to give it up. That's fine if they have met their commitment to the team or organization (don't allow your teens to quit in the middle of a season or term) and the activity isn't a good match with what you know of your kids' abilities, interests, and potential. But don't allow your teenagers to drop out of everything.

To brainstorm about possible areas for involvement, think in terms of the balanced life. In other words, consider how your teens are developing in the four main areas of life: physical, mental, social, and spiritual.

Physical activities include not only interscholastic sports but also intramurals, aerobics, church leagues, and YMCA workouts and leagues. What are your teenagers doing to develop in the physical area?

Obviously the mental area includes school—required classes, homework, and grades—which must be a high priority. But also consider the artistic side: drama, art, creative writing, and music. Middle school and high schools will offer many opportunities, but here again, involvement in this area doesn't have to be confined to the school. Check out private lessons, community groups, and church choirs. What are your teenagers doing apart from their academic classes to develop in the mental area?

Many social needs can be met through activities in the other areas (for example, interaction with teammates, choir members, and classmates), but special programs and activities focus on social needs. These include tutoring, student council, social committees, and many clubs. What are your teenagers doing to develop socially?

NO OPTION TO QUIT

I like the approach a mentor of mine took with his kids. Whenever they expressed interest in a new activity, the parents said, "Fine, but you must agree to stick with it for at least a year," or some other reasonable amount of time. Whenever the child would whine or try to give up on an activity before the agreed-on time had expired, he would say, "Sorry—no option to quit."

—Daryl Lucas
author of *The Eager Reader Bible* and the father of three boys

The spiritual area would involve church, Sunday school, youth group, specialized youth ministries such as Campus Life, and many others (see chapter 3). What are your teenagers doing to develop spiritually?

The goal should not be to keep your teenagers as busy as possible but to help them learn more about themselves and to develop in all areas of life.

Push Where You Must . . . But Be Willing to Compromise

Don't be afraid to push and insist on involvement when necessary. For example, teenagers should be required to stay on the team and stick it out for the rest of the season. If you encounter resistance, explain to your teenagers that they don't have a choice in the matter, but that they can choose their attitude. Use weather as an example: we cannot do anything to change rain into sunshine, but we can choose our attitudes during the rainy day. We can gripe, whine, complain, and generally make everyone around us miserable, or we can choose a positive attitude and make the most of a less-than-desirable situation.

Determine your nonnegotiables on the basis of your values and priorities, and be willing to give up, trade, and compromise in less important areas. If, for example, your high school daughter announces that she doesn't want to play basketball anymore (after four successful seasons in junior high and high school and a number of expensive basketball camps in the summer), you may want to scream, wonder what's wrong with her, or at least argue the point. But if you can get over your emotional involvement with the sport and potential embarrassment with parents of other team members, try to look at the situation objectively, honestly considering the relative importance of basketball in your daughter's life and future. You may discover that she could better invest her talents elsewhere. Instead of overreacting, talk through the situation with your daughter and work with her on choosing another venue for expending her time and energy.

Allow your teenagers to trade one area of involvement for another. You may say, for example, that they may stop taking piano lessons if they continue to develop their musical talents in another way. Or you could allow them to discontinue involvement in student council because of the increasing demands on their time from another, more important activity.

Look for ways to compromise, always working to build your teens' self-esteem and to discover their hidden talents and abilities.

Look for Alternatives

When we think of extracurricular activities, usually school sports, choirs, plays, student council, and various clubs come to mind. But many other options offer great opportunities for your teenagers. Often some of the less visible activities—the debate team, the school newspaper, the yearbook, sports trainer—can be fun and can provide valuable learning experiences. Our town's high school has a radio station and a bank, both run by students.

Many other opportunities exist off campus. Check out your church, park district, and other community resources for service groups, voice lessons, summer swim teams, tennis lessons, and so forth. I know one dad who encouraged his son to take up fishing, and the boy has excelled. Another father and son restore antique furniture together.

Use your imagination and search for creative options for getting your teenagers involved.

Build "Affirm" Foundation

Look for ways to affirm your teenagers. To begin with, you can show your respect by attending events in which they are participating. Often parents drop their kids off, pick them up, and never get out of the car. Go and take the time to learn more about your teens' activity. Learn from your adolescents. Then, look for specific points for affirmation. For example, during a game, look for positive moves, reactions, and results to compliment. Afterward you could say something like, "In the second period, that was a great move you made around the defender. And what a pass to the forward! How did you ever get that off?" Obviously you should not lie to your teenagers, making up undeserved statements of praise. But praise what you can. Be

EXPLORE ABILITIES

Your teenagers are coasting and taking the path of least resistance. The reason is clear: they're lazy and unmotivated, right? Not necessarily. Could it be that they are afraid? Perhaps the real problem is one of insecurity. Many young people have been so sheltered and underchallenged in their lives, they have no idea about what they're good at or where their abilities lie.

Expose your kids to all kinds of work and service opportunities. Let them try their hands at various hobbies. You may find that the son you've been futilely trying to make into a football star is, instead, a wonderfully talented woodcarver. And your daughter may be more suited to caring for small children than she is to dancing.

Help your children discover what God put them on this earth to do, and your days of nagging and prodding will be history. Nothing motivates like success.

—Len Woods
Minister to Students, Christ Community Church, Ruston, Louisiana

very specific about exactly what your teens did well. Generic "you were great" statements don't carry as much weight.

Also, do not qualify your affirmation with a "but," adding an area in which your teens need to improve. For example, you should *not* say something like, "You played very well, *but* you need to work on your dribbling." This statement includes a compliment (albeit a very general one), but the corrective ending undermines and almost entirely negates any affirmation. Most kids will focus on the last part of the statement and hear it as a criticism. Certainly kids need constructive criticism in order to improve, but that kind of helpful advice should come later. Most kids will be motivated to improve if they feel they are doing well.

Look for ways to celebrate successes. You could get ice cream, go out for a special dinner, or host a team or club party to encourage your kids' involvement in activities.

In addition to bolstering your teenagers' self-esteem, your affirmation will encourage them to keep practicing and improving in that activity. Because of my background in music, I used to point out mistakes in our daughter's piano playing as she practiced. I thought I was being helpful, but she resented my comments. No wonder she didn't want to practice when I was around. Lately I have been listening carefully and saying things like: "What is the name of that song? It's really beautiful." "There are some difficult chords in that piece. I'm amazed at how you can play them so well." "I love hearing you play the piano. It fills the house with music!" I believe that Dana has real potential in music, and I want her to continue to play the piano. My affirmation will encourage her to develop her God-given talent.

Adolescents need affirmation. Their tender egos need bolstering as they build self-esteem and identity. One of the *least* tough choices you can make as a loving parent is to give your teenagers your genuine praise.

* * *

Allowed to make all their own decisions about what they will do with their time, many adolescents will do very little at all and thus bury their talents and drift through the rest of their lives. As responsible parents, we need to help them discover and develop their God-given abilities and gifts, steering them toward a productive and rewarding future. You can do this by discovering your teenagers' unique abilities, insisting on their involvement in activities, pushing where necessary but being willing to compromise, looking for alternatives, and affirming them as special, talented, and much-loved people.

THINK IT THROUGH

1. For which of the following reasons have your adolescents dropped out of activities: tiredness, laziness, insecurity, discouragement?

2. When did your teenagers resist your efforts to get them involved in a specific activity? How did you react?

3. What special facts do you know about your teenagers, facts no one else knows about?

4. What personal unfulfilled desires and dreams may possibly push you to pressure your teens into certain activities?

5. What other adults could give you helpful information and insight about your kids?

6. What unique potential, talents, abilities, and gifts do your teenagers possess?

7. In what areas of life (physical, social, spiritual, mental) do your teens need to become more involved?

8. In what areas would you be willing to compromise with your adolescents and their activities?

9. What are some alternative, less-well-known lessons, sports, or classes in which your teens could get involved?

10. What can you do to affirm your teenagers as good and valuable human beings?

CHAPTER **10**

"I'll Think about the Future Later"

"You ought to help him out,
Dave. You're his big brother."
—Ozzie to David
from "The Speech"

"JACKIE, WHERE ARE you going at this hour?" Jan Draper puts down her book and calls to her teenage daughter as she hears Jackie begin to open the front door.

"Don't worry, Mom," Jackie calls back. "I'm just meeting Cheri and Ellie for dessert at PDQ Snacks. I'll be home before midnight."

"But it's a school night," her mom objects. "Do you have all your homework done?"

"No problem, Mom. I did it all during study hall," answers Jackie, quickly shutting the door behind her and walking into the night.

Wondering why her high school daughter has so little homework these days, Jan Draper gives a resigned shrug and returns to the book she was reading. Then, reflecting for a few minutes to when the older children (Bart, age twenty-two, and Sonia, age nineteen) were high school sophomores, Jan tries to remember their schedules and workload. Of course, that was a while ago, when Dick, her husband, was still around. So much has happened over those years. And since the divorce, Jan has had to scramble just to meet the family's physical, financial, and emotional needs. *Oh well,* she thinks, *I guess it's all right. Jackie's a good girl. She's passing, and she's not into any trouble or anything.*

Actually, Jackie told her mother the truth. She really doesn't have any schoolwork. But that's because her classes demand very little of her. Last spring, when putting together her schedule for the next year, Jackie chose a very easy course load, including a couple of study halls, and talked her mother into agreeing to it. In junior high, Jackie had shown promise in several areas and was even recommended for high school accelerated courses. But her friends and social life pushed studies to the periphery of her life. So this year she is no longer in the college track or even challenged in school. Jackie is content to slide through her classes.

As is the case with many moms and dads, especially single parents who are pressured, Jan Draper is satisfied with the fact that her daughter has nice friends and no major problems. With all the other pressures that Jan is feeling, the last thing she needs is to worry about her teenager.

The Challenge

The problem, however, is that without realizing it, Jackie is short-circuiting her future. But this fifteen-year-old is typical of many young people who focus on *now*. They are convinced that they can think about the future when it comes—much later.

In School

In several earlier chapters we discussed the importance of school, especially the fact that in addition to the subject matter, the classes and extracurricular activities teach young people much about themselves and help prepare them for careers and for life. School can be difficult. Good teachers make students think and work. And to most adolescents, school can seem long, tedious, and often boring. Kids would much rather hang out with friends, play sports, date, shop, eat, and generally have a good time.

With little concern for the years ahead, many teenagers can hardly wait to get out of school. They take the easy route and do as little as possible in junior high and senior high—just enough to get by. And in a startling number of cases, these teens drop out of school altogether.

Obviously, not everyone is cut out for college. But teenagers need a solid education to reach their potential, contribute to society, and make a difference in the world. Yet many kids think, "I don't need school. I can make enough money working at this job." So they go down that road and continue full speed in that direction, oblivious to the dead end around the bend.

In Relationships

This tendency to focus on present pleasure and to live for *now* can also be seen in teenage relationships. In chapter 2 we took a close look at dating and discussed the growing pressure on young people to date early and to be sexually active.

The words *intense* and *urgent* epitomize young love. Driven by needs for affirmation, affection, and attention, adolescents are drawn to each other like iron to magnets. With their increasingly powerful sex drive and mysterious new feelings for the opposite sex added to the mix, young teens make numerous awkward attempts at romance. During the junior high years, sex organs develop, pubic hair appears, boys begin to masturbate, girls begin to menstruate, and both begin to talk dirty and act cool. At the same time, teens are barraged by movies, television shows, videos, music, and disc jockeys that promote sexual activity. Confused about their feelings yet wanting to be "in" and act older, they pair up and often become physically involved.

If, as Freud proposed, maturity is the ability to postpone gratification, then adolescents in love demonstrate gross *immaturity.* Sexual feelings demand expression *now.* Waiting seems impossible. Thus, many high school couples talk about getting married. Others may not discuss marriage but suddenly find themselves facing pregnancy and many difficult decisions. Whatever the outcome, these young people have traded their *tomorrows* for what they can get *today.*

In Values

What holds the number one spot in the life of a typical middle school student? Many kids would answer, "friends." As we have discussed in other chapters, during adolescence, friends become all-consuming and all-important. Kids will take incredible risks and make foolish choices just to please the crowd because their highest priority is to be liked and accepted. With little or no thought of the future, they make what can turn out to be life-changing or even life-threatening decisions for *present* rewards.

In high school this trend continues, though the emphasis shifts slightly toward being popular. Think back to your high school days. Remember the "in" crowd? Every high school has one. Usually composed of cheerleaders, star athletes, and other older students, the in crowd had power in the school. They were the popular kids who made things happen. If you belonged to that group, you basked in your status. High school was fun for you and perhaps has even been the high point of your life to this point. If you were not a member of that privileged in group, you may remember longing to be accepted by those power brokers, to join that small circle of beautiful people. Now, when considering whether to attend a high school reunion, you think of how you would like to look and act, to show *them* that although you weren't in during those four years, you have succeeded since then.

Kids still want to belong to the in crowd. Thus, with many high school students, popularity becomes almost an obsession, and they are willing to compromise nearly everything to gain that desired status. Christians hide their faith. Insecure teenagers take their first drink, egged on by others at the party. New drivers career recklessly to impress their teenage passengers. Kids smoke to look cool and to show their independence. Girls give in to sexual pressure from older boyfriends. Nearly everything can be sacrificed to this god of popularity.

With popularity crowding into the number one slot, all other values are pushed lower on the list of personal priorities.

In Planning

Can you imagine asking a four-year-old to plan the family vacation? With such limited knowledge, perspective, and experience, the plans no doubt would include idealistic activities, a ridiculous budget, and an impossible schedule.

Although adolescents are much more experienced and have a greater grasp of reality than a child of four, their understanding of the world is still severely limited. In fact, these kids are just beginning to put things together. To fulfill an assignment for a youth ministry class that I was teaching, two college students interviewed some eighth-grade girls in the Chicago suburbs. During the discussion, the junior high girls spoke freely about their relationships with guys, and one explained that recently she and her boyfriend had been talking about getting married in a few years. A minute later in the conversation, when one of the college students mentioned that her home was in Wisconsin, this same eighth-grade girl blurted out: "Do they have TV in Wisconsin?" This young girl had been talking about a serious, adult commitment—marriage, yet she didn't even know about life in a neighboring state.

This lack of experience and knowledge can lead to some very strange lifestyle choices and plans for the future. Kids will drop out of school to work or to get married. They will spend all their money on a stereo or car. They will choose a dead-end "career." They will smoke, drink, or take drugs with little thought about the possible consequences.

Adolescents tend to live only for the moment or for the next few days and weeks. In the process they cheat themselves and rob their futures.

The Conflict

Perhaps the greatest contributing cause of this problem is adolescents' perception of time. Elsewhere in this book, I have mentioned teenage misconceptions about life. This is the big one!

Relative Time

Although we human beings mark and measure time with specific units (years, months, days, hours, minutes, and seconds), the reality of time for each individual is how he or she perceives it. For example, the last five minutes in a boring class can seem like an eternity; yet the last five minutes in an exciting basketball game, when your team is behind, can seem to disappear in the blink of an eye.

To illustrate this another way, consider this question: Is life long or short? If a man lives to be eighty years old, usually we say that he has lived a long life. But ask that eighty-year-old if his life has been long, and he is likely to say, "It has gone by very quickly." The length-of-life answer depends on one's perspective. And in light of all human history or in light of eternity, our lives are short indeed. James reminds us: "What is your life? You are a mist that appears for a little while and then vanishes" (James 4:14).

Now, think of how long a year feels to a five-year-old girl. Although a year is composed of 365 days for her, just as for everyone else, one year represents *twenty percent* of that little girl's life. So when her mother says, "Grandpa will be visiting us in about a year," to the little girl, that length of time may as well be 100 years because it's too long for her to comprehend.

THE ENIGMA OF TIME

Ask six people to explain time today, and, like the six blind men poking the elephant, you may get six answers. A physicist may say time is one of the two basic building blocks of the universe, the other being space. For a clockmaker time is the ticktock of his handiwork. For a science fiction fan it is the fourth dimension. A biologist sees time in the internal clocks that keep plants and animals in sync with nature. For a banker it is money. . . .

"We have given more attention to measuring time than to anything in nature," says Gernot Winkler, Director of Time Services at the U.S. Naval Observatory in Washington, D.C. "But time remains an abstraction, a riddle that exists only in our minds."

—John Boslough
"The Enigma of TIME"[1]

During history class, my eighth-grade teacher commented that an important historical event had occurred "only ten years ago." I remember thinking in my thirteen-year-old mind, *"Only* ten years! That's a *long* time, not an 'only'!" I was right because at that time, ten years would have been more than two-thirds of my lifetime. These days, of course, like that history teacher, I often speak of "only ten years ago." Today, a decade is no big deal, and I can remember many events of the mid-eighties as if they happened yesterday.

Carrying this one step further, in high school a friend told me that he was planning to be a doctor someday. I asked how long he would have to go to school to achieve his goal. He responded, "About nine years after we graduate." To me, as a high school senior, that seemed either impossible to attain or very unrealistic. Nine years was half of the time I had been alive; I couldn't comprehend spending that long in school. As it turned out, with college and seminary, I ended up going to school for eight years after high school, nearly as long as my friend had suggested.

As you can see, time is relative. In fact, the older a person becomes, the faster time seems to move because each year that passes is a smaller portion of that person's lifetime.

Generation Gap

This difference in perceiving time contributes to many conflicts between generations. Older people have the benefit of having lived many years and can see the big picture. Whether from looking back at their foolish, youthful mistakes or just realizing how quickly time passes, men and women in their thirties, forties, fifties, and beyond understand the importance of having patience and of preparing for the future. I have spoken with many adults who remember their high school years with regret, wishing that they had participated in different activities, had taken other courses, had studied more, and had made a difference for Christ. Others made poor, immature choices for which they are still suffering the consequences. These adults want to tell adolescents, especially their own, "Don't make the mistake I made!" But it's difficult for kids to understand and appreciate their message.

Youthful Thoughts

This unique perception of time and very limited perspective leads to two predominant youthful ideas about time and life.

The first is an almost overpowering emphasis on the present tense—*now*. Because ten years is a *very* long time to teenagers, most find it nearly impossible to plan that far in advance. Yet the message they hear from adults, especially parents, teachers, youth leaders, and others who care about them is to *wait*. Even waiting for a short time can be tough, but they are told to wait a few years to vote, to drive a car, to have sex, and to realize other *adult* activities, privileges, and experiences. If something feels good, they want to do it right away and not have to wait.

In addition, our society's escalating emphasis on getting information, answers, and service faster and faster heightens the expectations to have everything immediately. In chapter 6, we discussed how modern technology has quickened and busied the pace of life. Microwave ovens, fast-food restaurants with drive-through windows, overnight mail-order companies, E-mail, on-line services, and other advances seem to make waiting obsolete.

This makes it tough to convince adolescents to postpone sexual gratification ("wait until marriage"), to put off getting a job and build a solid educational foundation for a meaningful career, and to work hard today for a future reward. Most teenagers live for the present.

PLANNING FOR THE FUTURE

Two experiments can help teach your teenager the benefits of long-term planning and the drawbacks of living for the moment.

1. If you can afford it, give your adolescent a lump sum of money from which he or she is to purchase all clothing and personal effects for the entire school year. Explain the "how tos" of the budgeting process. Strongly encourage the practice of saving money for "down the road." Express clearly the fact that "this is all you get. Once it's gone, there is no more." In the end, you will probably end up with a broke (and a broken!) teen, but your son or daughter will remember the lesson for a long time.

2. Embark on a long-term project with your teen. It might be restoring an old car or turning an attic or basement into a bedroom. Whatever the case, the experience of working together over a long period of time in order to see the desired results will make a lasting impression.

—Len Woods
Minister to Students, Christ Community Church, Ruston, Louisiana

The second idea that young people have about the relationship of time to life is that time is on their side. In other words, because thirty or forty years seems like an endless amount of time, they believe it will take a long time to get there. Thus, when discussing profound issues, such as their relationship with God, kids will often say, "I'll worry about that later, when I'm old. Right now I don't want to be so serious."

Because of this, adolescents find it difficult to project their lives very far into the future. People who are thirty years old seem ancient to many teens, even though they have parents, grandparents, teachers, coaches, and others who are well beyond that decade. Adults can lecture teenagers about how certain habits such as cigarette smoking will shorten a person's life. Usually, however, those arguments bounce right off. Kids aren't going to worry about what they can't imagine. "Anyway, what's a year or two?" they reply.

Actually, teenagers subconsciously believe that they are immortal. Death isn't real to them. They feel good; they are strong and fast; they can see well; the end of life seems far away. So kids smoke, drink, take drugs, drive under the influence of alcohol or drugs, and engage in many other risky behaviors, truly believing that nothing can happen to them. And many die.

Believing that now is all that counts and that time is on their side, many young people make very foolish decisions and gamble with their lives.

So, What's a Parent to Do?

When discussing addiction and codependency, professional counselors describe "enablers," people who by their action or inaction allow self-destructive behavior to continue in the addicted or dependent person. Most parents would vehemently deny that they are enablers, that they encourage their kids to be shortsighted and to mortgage the future for the present. But many do.

Some are too busy to get involved in their kids' lives. Many know what they should do but don't have the courage to make the tough choices that we have discussed throughout this book. Others simply don't like conflict and try to avoid it at any cost. Whatever the reason, these parents allow their sons and daughters to drift into the future, unprepared for relationships, careers, and adult life.

The Choice

The task here is formidable—trying to help young people see what they can't even imagine. That is, your goal should be to help your teenagers catch a glimpse of the big picture. This will be difficult, and with some teens it will be impossible. But here's what you can do.

Talk/Teach

With every tough choice you have to make, especially those that relate directly to the future, you should explain to your adolescents that you are in the parenting business for the long haul. (Teenagers will have to be reminded several times of this truth.) That is, you love them deeply and want the very best for their lives. And you aren't going to stop loving them during arguments, stress, problems, and failures. Your love is unconditional, *but it's not always pleasant.* Sometimes you will have to insist on their obedience to rules and their compliance to your wishes. This also means that you are very concerned about what kind of adults they will be ten, twenty, and even thirty years from now. You're not just worried about how they are doing at this moment, today.

Explain that at times they won't understand what you want or your reasons for your decisions. It's good for them to ask questions, to look for answers and explanations. Explain that you will listen carefully and will compromise when possible. But eventually they will have to trust you and your decision. They will have to trust that you are wise and have their best interests at heart.

In addition to explaining your reasoning and the necessity for trust, you can point your children to Scripture, to those passages that speak of time, stewardship, and values, such as Psalm 39:5-7; Proverbs 1:8-9, 20-33; 3:3-6; 24:14; Matthew 6:25-34; Ephesians 5:15-17; James 4:13-16.

One of the most powerful biblical stories is the life of Solomon. Explain that Solomon had it all: power, riches beyond imagination, and all that money could buy. Yet he blew it; he allowed money, sex, and power to take God's place in his life. As a result, he saw his life unravel. In the book of Ecclesiastes, Solomon summarizes his experiences and presents wise and powerful lessons about how we should order our lives. Ecclesiastes 11:9–12:1 states: "Young man, it's wonderful to be young! Enjoy every minute of it! Do all you want to; take in everything, but realize that you must account to God for everything you do. So banish grief and pain, but remember that youth, with a whole life before it, can make serious mistakes. Don't let the excitement of being young cause you to forget about your Creator. Honor him in your youth before the evil years come—when you'll no longer enjoy living" (TLB).

Then Solomon goes on to describe the realities of old age: pain, fear, frailty, and, for a person without God, bitterness. Solomon ends this book with his strong summary of how people should live in light of eternity: "Here is my final conclusion: fear God and obey his commandments, for this is the entire duty of man. For

God will judge us for everything we do, including every hidden thing, good or bad" (Ecclesiastes 12:13-14, TLB).

The lesson is clear: The decisions we make when we are young will determine the kind of people we will become. If we begin well, the chances are good that we will end well.

Another resource for helping your teenagers understand time, priorities, and the importance of making the right choices is the testimonies of other people. Often children become so used to hearing their parents give advice that they don't really listen. Teenagers who are moving toward independence will try hard to shut their parents out of their lives. But you know of many other adults who love your kids and whom your kids respect. Enlist their help. Ask them to share, at an appropriate time, their experiences and counsel. Don't make this a formal interview, but look for ways to give these adults opportunities to tell their stories. You could have a respected teacher or your pastor over for dinner; you could ask a family friend to write your son or daughter a personal letter; you could ask the youth director to discuss the issue during a youth group meeting. Young adults, college students, and those in their twenties will be very effective because they aren't that far removed from high school. But senior citizens will have much to share as well, especially through their stories. Often teens will be more open to insights and guidance from an *outsider* than from their parents.

Don't overwhelm your kids with a barrage of information and testimonials, but use all your resources to communicate this message to them. It's that important.

Insist
Obviously, the ideal is that your teenagers will make the right decisions on their own, assisted by your interesting and effective teaching. But they may not be convinced and may seem deter-

mined to make poor choices that you know will hurt their future. That is when you will have to insist on other, more responsible courses of action.

Last summer, as a mother and father were discussing the next year's high school courses and schedule, their freshman son gave an impassioned plea against taking chemistry and accelerated English. He had all the reasons you may expect, and he presented them very convincingly (his friends were taking the easier courses; he didn't need those courses to get into college; he would feel better about himself if he got an A in another class rather than a B or C in the tougher one; he needed more time for football, choir, and his spiritual life—it was hard to ignore that one). Knowing their son well, this mom and dad insisted that he take the more difficult courses, over his complaints, protests, and dire predictions of failure. They also explained that the decision had been made and that he should choose a positive attitude and make the most of it. The next year, their sophomore son flourished in those classes and has even stated that they are his favorites. Wisely, his parents didn't remind him of their summer argument and say, "We told you so."

Certainly not all parent-child confrontations will turn out that positively. Many kids will sulk, act defiantly, disobey, and even rebel. Others may allow themselves to fail in order to prove their parents wrong. And, of course, some parents may be wrong in their evaluation of their teens' abilities. Yet those possibilities should not deter you from making this tough choice. If you and your spouse are convinced of a certain course of action that will have great future impact, then insist on it. Don't allow them to date at age fourteen; insist on the college prep track; make family and church a priority; enforce the curfew; say no to the job. Have the courage to do what you know you must. Remember, you have a mature, adult perspective on time and life. You know what's ahead and the road that leads there.

Faced with very difficult situations and conflicts with their kids, some parents have had their teens change schools or have even moved to another state. A measure like that would be extreme, but it may have to happen, as a last resort.

Don't let your children throw away their future because they want pleasure now.

* * *

Motivated by their lack of perspective, misunderstanding of time, and the excitement of being young, young people live for the present. They want everything now and often will sacrifice their future to get it. Responsible parents who love their children hold them back, teach them to wait, and steer them in the right direction. Don't deny your kids their tomorrows by allowing them to make foolish decisions today. Make the tough choice to teach them the lessons you have learned and the principles of Scripture.

THINK IT THROUGH

1. What evidence do you see that your adolescents want to live for now—in school? in relationships? in values? in planning?
2. When did you first become aware that time passes quickly and that life is short?
3. How did that awareness affect your life?
4. What regrets do you have about your youthful decisions?
5. When have your teenagers shown extreme impatience?
6. What have you done to enable your teens' poor decision making?
7. When will you take the time to talk to your adolescents about time and preparing for the future?
8. When will you discuss Solomon and Ecclesiastes together with your teens?
9. What adult friends will you enlist in this teaching project?
10. How and when can they help?
11. What decisions and choices will you have to insist on with your teens in the near future?

EPILOGUE

Life's experiences teach many lessons. Perhaps the most difficult lesson is that love can be painful.

Love's pain is felt most deeply by parents with their children. For many years parents give to their kids, spending money and time to help them mature, spending emotional energy to bandage skinned knees, to console broken hearts, and to pray at their side in the hospital.

Investing themselves daily, loving moms and dads also teach, guide, and discipline. "This hurts me more than it hurts you" may be a cliché repeated by generations of parents while punishing a wayward child, but it's true. Loving mothers and fathers don't enjoy saying no and correcting bad behavior; it would be much easier to let the child wander any chosen path. But, motivated by love, these parents endure inconvenience, pain, conflicts, and the inevitable screams of "I hate you!" to steer their children in the right direction. To be a good parent—loving and responsible—means being vulnerable, open to being wounded and scared, making tough choices with kids. Love hurts.

In this book, I have described ten important areas in which responsible parents must make tough choices with their teenagers. They are *tough* because these choices are difficult to make, often going against the current of popular opinion and usually causing conflict with the child. Undoubtedly the teenage years comprise the most difficult era of parenting. With changing, growing, and maturing bodies and minds, adolescents assault the boundaries and push for independence. Yet these are also undoubtedly the most critical years. The decisions and experiences during the adolescent years affect your teenagers for life. Although these choices are tough, they are vitally important.

As you move through this decade of parenting each child, I pray that you will have the courage and strength to do what you know you must despite the pain. Make these tough choices with your teenagers regarding friends, dating, faith, television, entertainment, values, school, money and work, talents, and preparing for the future. It will affect them for the rest of their lives.

"Is your life full of difficulties and temptations? Then be happy, for when the way is rough, your patience has a chance to grow. So let it grow, and don't try to squirm out of your problems. For when your patience is finally in full bloom, then you will be ready for anything, strong in character, full and complete. If you want to know what God wants you to do, ask him, and he will gladly tell you, for he is always ready to give a bountiful supply of wisdom to all who ask him; he will not resent it" (James 1:2-5, TLB).

RESOURCES

Books

50 Practical Ways to Take Our Kids Back from the World by Michael J. McManus (Wheaton, Ill.: Tyndale House Publishers, 1993). This easy-to-read-and-use paperback is jammed with helpful counsel and workable ideas.

From Dad, with Love by Chuck Aycock and Dave Veerman. (Wheaton, Ill.: Tyndale, 1994). This extremely practical book, written by two veteran youth experts and fathers, explains how dads can give their kids gifts that money can't buy.

Getting Ready for the Guy/Girl Thing by Greg Johnson and Susie Shellenberger (Ventura, Calif.: Regal Books, 1991). This practical book gives advice to junior high students on dating and just getting along with the opposite sex.

Getting Your Kid to Talk by Dave Veerman (Wheaton, Ill.: Tyndale, 1994). This book offers 101 practical ideas (plus bonus ideas) for starting or deepening conversation with children of all ages.

Helping Teens in Crisis by Miriam Neff (Wheaton, Ill.: Tyndale, 1993). Written by a Christian counselor who works daily with scores of high school kids, this valuable resource for parents and youthworkers focuses on teens who struggle with divorce, self-esteem, school, substance abuse, and other crises.

How to Apply the Bible by Dave Veerman (Wheaton, Ill.: Tyndale, 1993). This book is an inexpensive, easy-to-read book filled with proven techniques for discovering the truths of Scripture and putting them into practice today.

Learn to Discern by Robert G. DeMoss Jr. (Grand Rapids: Zondervan, 1992). This outstanding analysis of popular culture and the battle over values includes a book and companion video (same title), each providing practical steps that parents can take to protect their children and help them to think critically.

Life Application Bible for Students (Wheaton, Ill.: Tyndale, 1992). This exciting resource for junior high and senior high young people draws them into God's Word and helps them apply it to their lives. Notes and features include book introductions, Personality Profiles, Moral Dilemma notes, "I Wonder" notes, "Here's What I Did" notes, Ultimate Issues notes, Life Application notes, Megathemes and discussion questions for each book, maps, charts, highlighted memory verses, Bible reading plan, "Appointments with God" follow-up plan for new believers, Where to Find It index, and Life-Changer Index.

Love, Sex, and Dating series by Barry St. Clair and Bill Jones (Wheaton, Ill.: Victor Books, 1993). Excellent books for kids and resources for youth leaders. The series contains the following books: *Dating: Going Out in Style; Love: Making it Last; Sex: Desiring the Best; Talking with Your Kids about Love, Sex, and Dating;* and *Leader's Guide* (written by Tim Atkins, Vince Morris, and Gene DiPaolo).

Margin by Richard A. Swenson, M.D. (Colorado Springs: NavPress, 1992). This book offers a healing prescription for dealing with the overload of modern society, helping men and women find and create much needed emotional, physical, financial, and time reserves.

Parenting Passages by David R. Veerman (Wheaton, Ill.: Tyndale, 1994). This book offers invaluable information and counsel to help parents safely navigate through all eleven critical stages of parenting.

Raising Money-Smart Kids: How to Teach Your Children the Secrets of Earning, Saving, Investing, and Spending Wisely by Ron and Judy Blue (Nashville: Thomas Nelson, 1992). This practical books helps parents teach children of all ages money-management skills that will help them throughout their lives.

Reaching Out to Troubled Youth by Dwight Spotts and David Veerman (Wheaton, Ill.: Victor Books, 1994) This intensely practical and power-packed book seeks to motivate, encourage, and help those working with young people who have critical needs.

Ready for Life series by Dave Veerman, et. al. (Wheaton, Ill.: Victor Books, 1994). This six-volume series of active life-skills curricula for junior highers, written by eight experts in the field, covers *How to Be a Good Friend, How to Get Along with the Opposite Sex, How to Teach Your Parents, How to Win in Life, How to Know What God Wants,* and *How to Explain What You Believe.* It is ideal for use in Sunday school, youth group, or home.

Today's Music: A Window to Your Child's Soul by Al Menconi (Elgin, Ill.: David C. Cook, 1990). This book is an excellent summary of contemporary music, with practical advice on how parents can take positive, helpful action.

Understanding Today's Youth Culture by Walt Mueller (Wheaton, Ill.: Tyndale, 1994). This "complete guide for parents, teachers, and youth leaders" contains an in-depth look at characteristics of teenagers, change, music, media, peers, love, sex, materialism, alcohol, and drugs.

Video Movies Worth Watching by Dave Veerman (Grand Rapids: Baker, 1992). This book, which reviews seventy-five videos and provides discussion questions and suggestions for use, is an excellent resource for parents and youthworkers for stimulating discussion with young people.

Magazines and Newsletters

Alpha-Omega Film Report. This monthly newsletter gives valuable information about new motion picture and video releases. Each issue reviews the latest secular films, detailing plots and themes, critiquing production quality and acting, and highlighting objectionable content. Subscriptions cost $12.50 and may be ordered by writing to Alpha-Omega Productions, P.O. Box 25605, Colorado Springs, CO 80936.

Breakaway and *Brio*. These magazines from Focus on the Family are written specifically for junior high students (*Breakaway* for boys, *Brio* for girls). The magazines are loaded with stories, columns, cartoons, and other features designed to inspire, instruct, and entertain. For more information, write to Focus on the Family, P.O. Box 35500, Colorado Springs, CO 80935-3550, or call 719/531-3400.

Campus Life. This outstanding Christian magazine for high school students contains stories of kids and other articles centering on the problems and needs of young people. Regular columns focus on personal Bible study, contemporary music, humor, and communicating Christ. A special college edition is published twice a year. To subscribe, write to *Campus Life*, 465 Gundersen Drive, Carol Stream, IL 60188, or call 800/678-6083.

CCM (Contemporary Christian Music) Magazine. This monthly publication features insightful and provocative articles, interviews with Christian artists, reviews of current performances and albums, and previews of new releases. To subscribe, write to CCM Publications, 107 Kenner Ave., Nashville, TN 37205.

Media Update. This bimonthly magazine of Al Menconi Ministries provides challenging commentaries and helpful analyses of contemporary music, artists, movies, and videos from a distinctively Christian perspective. To subscribe, write to *Media Update*, P.O. Box 5008, San Marcos, CA 92069-1050, or call 619/591-4696.

MOVIEGUIDE. This guide is a ministry of Good News Communications, whose stated purpose is "to redeem the values of the mass media." Published every two weeks, the guide provides reviews and analyses of current films and television shows. The goal is to help Christians understand movies and entertainment from a biblical perspective so they can choose the good and reject the bad. To subscribe or to receive more information, write to *MOVIEGUIDE,* P.O. Box 9952, Atlanta, GA 30319.

Preview. This newsletter, which is published twice each month by Movie Morality Ministries, summarizes, analyzes, and rates current movies. Each movie preview contains a concise summary covering these areas: Crude Language, Obscene Language, Profanity, Violence, Sexual Intercourse/Nudity, Homosexual Conduct, Sexually Suggestive Dialogue/Action, Drug Abuse, Other, and Intended Audience. This is an excellent resource for parents. To obtain more information or to subscribe, write to *Preview,* 1309 Seminole Drive, Richardson, TX 75080, or call 214/231-9910.

Movies and Videos

Life on the Edge. This Focus on the Family video series helps young people prepare for the challenges of adulthood. Hosted by Dr. James Dobson, the topics include: *Finding God's Will for Your Life, The Myth of Safe Sex, Love Must Be Tough, The Keys to Lifelong Love, When God Doesn't Make Sense, Pornography: Addictive, Progressive and Deadly,* and *Emotions: Can You Trust Them?* Each video is approximately fifty minutes in length. Available at Christian bookstores.

Gospel Films. This is one of the oldest and most well-respected Christian film producers and distributors, with perhaps the most extensive collection of Christian movies and videos available. For more information, write to Gospel Films, P.O. Box 455, Muskegon, MI 49443-0455 or phone 616/773-3361.

McCullough Family Media, Inc. This company provides a variety of Christian values–oriented films that entertain all ages. They produce their own movies, distribute others, and publish a monthly newsletter/order form. For more information, write to McCullough Family Media, Inc., 2924 Knight St., Shreveport, LA 71105.

Seminars

Understanding Your Teenager. This one-day seminar for parents is taught by Wayne Rice (writer, speaker, and cofounder of Youth Specialties) or another well-known youth expert. For more information and scheduling, write to Understanding Your Teenager, 10928 Vista Camino, Lakeside, CA 92040.

Ministry Organizations

Christian Camping International. CCI publishes a listing of over 750 Christian camps in the United States as well as contracts in eleven other countries. Listing includes family camps, sport camps, and camps for troubled teenagers or teenagers with disabilities. Fee is charged for listing. For more information, write to Christian Camping International, P.O. Box 62189, Colorado Springs, CO 80962-2189, or phone 719/260-9400.

Fellowship of Christian Athletes. This ministry to athletes is led by Christian coaches who meet with students in Huddle groups. FCA also sponsors camps, events, and conferences. For more information, write to Fellowship of Christian Athletes, 8701 Leeds Road, Kansas City, MO 64129, or phone 816/921-0909.

Student Venture. The high school ministry of Campus Crusade for Christ, SV is active in several metropolitan areas across America. The main focus of SV is to train students to reach their friends for Christ. For more information, write Student Venture, Campus Crusade for Christ, 100 Sunport Lane, Orlando, FL 32809, or phone 407/826-2150.

Young Life. This pioneer in relational ministry focuses primarily on junior high and high school students through Young Life clubs and a strong camping program. For more information, write to Young Life, P.O. Box 520, Colorado Springs, CO 80901, or phone 719/473-4262.

Youth for Christ. This interdenominational organization ministers to high school and junior high school students through personal counseling, Campus Life clubs, camps, trips, large events, and conventions. Professional staff spend many hours each week on the campuses, building relationships with kids. For more information, write to Youth for Christ, P.O. Box 228822, Denver, CO 80222, or phone 303/843-9000.

The Dove Foundation. This watchdog group screen movies and videos to determine their acceptability for family viewing. In the newsletter *In Flight,* Dove lists family-approved films and videos as well as the video stores that display the Dove Seal on their family-approved movies. To add your name to the Dove mailing list, write The Dove Foundation, 4521 Broadmoor SE, Grand Rapids, MI 49512-5339, or phone 800/218-DOVE(3683).

Missions Trips

ADVENTURES IN MISSIONS
    437 Brenau Avenue
    Gainesville, GA 30501
    800/881-AIM1

MISSION DISCOVERY
    P.O. Box 1073
    Hendersonville, TN 37077-1073

PIONEERS (World Outreach Fellowship merged with this organization)
SPRINT (short-term missions project name)
12343 Narcoossee Road
Orlando, FL 32827
407/382-6000

PROJECT SERVE
Youth for Christ/USA; Attn: Larry Williams
P.O. Box 228822
Denver, CO 80222
303/843-9000

REIGN MINISTRIES (Corporate Name)
ROYAL SERVANTS INTERNATIONAL. This multi-week street evangelism ministry includes two weeks of training, then overseas to Great Britain, Europe, Russia, etc., teaching students how to disciple and share their faith.

YOUTH ADVENTURES. This small mentoring ministry for troubled boys also includes missions trips for youth groups and pastors. For more information about these ministries, write to Reign Ministries, 5517 Warwick Place, Minneapolis, MN 55436-2467, or phone 612/823-4050.

Short Term Missions Handbook (1992), will be updated in 1997
The Great Commission Handbook (updated yearly)
Missions Today (updated yearly)
Berry Publishing Services
701 Main Street
Evanston, IL 60202
847/869-1573

SON SHINE MINISTRIES INTERNATIONAL
P.O. Box 456
Azle, TX 76098-0456
817/444-3777

TEEN MISSIONS INTERNATIONAL
885 East Hall Rd.
Merritt Island, FL 32953-8443
407/453-0350

YOUTH WITH A MISSION
7085 Battle Creek Road SE
Salem, OR 97301
503/364-3837

NOTES

Chapter 1—"Friends Are My Life!"
1. Quentin J. Schultze in an interview with Paul Galloway, *Chicago Tribune*, 10 March 1995.
2. Len Kageler, *Helping Your Teenager Cope with Peer Pressure* (Loveland, Colo.: Group Books, 1989), 184, 186.
3. Ibid., 184.

Chapter 2—"I Need a Date to Homecoming"
1. *Source*, (Search Institute) 4, no. 3 (July 1989): 3.
2. Chuck Aycock and Dave Veerman, *From Dad, with Love* (Wheaton, Ill.: Tyndale, 1994), 130–1.
3. For general information about the *True Love Waits* campaign, call 800/588-9246. To order materials, call 615/251-2772, or write Customer Service Center, Baptist Sunday School Board, 127 Ninth Ave. North, Nashville, TN 37234.

Chapter 3—"Church? . . . Boring!"
1. *Source* (Search Institute) 6, no. 2 (June 1990): 2.
2. *America's Youth in the 1990s* (The George H. Gallup International Institute, 1993), 153.
3. Mark DeVries, *Family-Based Youth Ministry* (Downer's Grove, Ill.: InterVarsity Press, 1994), 150–1.
4. Dean Merrill, *Wait Quietly: Devotions for a Busy Parent* (Wheaton, Ill.: Tyndale, 1994), 20.

Chapter 4—"Whoever Has the Remote Has the Power"
1. Jane Delano Brown et al., *Communication Research* (February 1990): 72.
2. Judith Waldrop, *American Demographics Marketing Tools* (February 1993): 13.
3. Quentin J. Schultze, *Redeeming Television* (Downers Grove, Ill.: InterVarsity Press, 1992), 46.

4. *USA Today,* 30 November 1989.
5. Newton Minow, *Consumer Reports* (March 1995): 160.
6. Sylvia Skarstad, "View from the Chalkboard," *Youthworker* (winter 1995): 71.
7. Reported in the *Chicago Tribune,* 18 February 1995.
8. Reported in *TV Guide,* 22 August 1992.
9. Reported in *Newsweek,* 12 July 1993.
10. Reported in the *Chicago Tribune,* 18 February 1995.
11. Ibid.
12. Reported in *U.S. News & World Report,* 10 October 1994.
13. Neil Postman, *Amusing Ourselves to Death* (New York: Penguin Books, 1985), 78.
14. Walt Mueller, *Understanding Today's Youth Culture* (Wheaton, Ill.: Tyndale, 1994), 124–5.
15. Dennis A. Britton, *Chicago Sun-Times* editorial, 7 March 1995.
16. Quentin J. Schultze, *Dancing in the Dark* (Grand Rapids: Eerdmans, 1991), 76–7.

Chapter 5—"Pump Up the Volume"
1. Robert DeMoss Jr., *Learn to Discern* (Grand Rapids: Zondervan, 1992), 61.
2. Michael Medved, *Hollywood vs. America* (New York: HarperCollins, 1992), 10.
3. DeMoss, *Learn to Discern,* 61.
4. David Veerman, *Parenting Passages* (Wheaton, Ill.: Tyndale, 1994), 58.
5. Al Menconi, *Media Update* 13, no. 4.
6. Al Menconi, *Today's Music: A Window to Your Child's Soul* (Elgin, Ill.: David C. Cook, 1990), 67.
7. Michael Medved, *Hollywood vs. America: Popular Culture and the War against Traditional Values* (San Francisco: HarperCollins, 1992), 23.
8. DeMoss, *Learn to Discern,* 85.
9. Al Menconi, *Media Update* 10, no. 2, 1–2.

Chapter 6—"I'm Too Busy to Sleep"
1. "Teens and Technology: Together for Life," *YOUTHviews* 2, no. 3, (November 1994): 4.
2. Steven Waldman, *The New Republic,* 27 January 1992.
3. David Elkind, *All Grown Up & No Place to Go* (Reading, Mass.: Addison-Wesley, 1984), 4.
4. Kevin Leenhouts, *Campus Life Magazine* (February 1976): 20.
5. Sylvia Skarstad, "View from the Chalkboard," *Youthworker* (winter 1995): 71–2.
6. Richard A. Swenson, M.D., *Margin* (Colorado Springs: NavPress, 1992), 66–7.
7. Ibid., 145.

8. Ibid., 161.
9. Kay Linskoog, *The Other Side* (May/June 1976): 49.

Chapter 7—"School . . . Who Needs It?"
1. *Source* (Search Institute) 10, no. 3 (October 1994): 1.
2. Sylvia Skarstad, "View from the Chalkboard" *Youthworker* (winter 1995): 73.

Chapter 8—"But I Need Money"
1. George Barna, "Is Your Store Cool Enough?" *Bookstore Journal* (February 1991): 61.
2. Steve Wilstein, "Campuses Fertile Ground for Growing Gambling Epidemic," *Chicago Tribune*, 2 April 1995.
3. Sylvia Skarstad, "View from the Chalkboard," *Youthworker* (winter 1995): 71.
4. Ellen Greenberger and Laurence Steinberg, *When Teenagers Work* (New York: Basic Books, 1986), 6.
5. Jay Kesler, *Energizing Your Teenager's Faith* (Loveland, Colo.: Group Books, 1990).
6. Greenberger and Steinberg, *When Teenagers Work*, 118.
7. Ibid., 106.

Chapter 10—"I'll Think about the Future Later"
1. John Boslough, "The Enigma of TIME," *National Geographic* (March 1990): 109–10.

ABOUT THE AUTHOR

Dave and Gail Veerman live in Naperville, Illinois, with their two daughters, Kara and Dana. A graduate of Wheaton College (B.A.) and Trinity Evangelical Divinity School (M.Div.), Dave ministered with Youth for Christ in Illinois and Louisiana for 26 years. Presently he is a partner in The Livingstone Corporation, a team of writers and editors. In addition to his work with Livingstone, Dave teaches, speaks, and is involved in the Naperville Presbyterian Church (PCA) as an elder, choir member, and junior high ministry leader. Dave has written more than thirty books—including *Parenting Passages, From Dad with Love,* and *Getting Your Kid to Talk*—and has edited several others, including the best-selling *Life Application Bible.* He is also heavily involved in the local high school, and he runs to keep in shape. Perhaps Dave's greatest claim to fame, however, is his ability to play his nose, which he has done in venues all over the world.